RUNNING THROUGH THE GRAVEYARD

*To Karen
God Bless you
Love
Tom
Phil 4:13*

Thomas J. Miranda

© 2016 Thomas J. Miranda

All Rights Reserved.

No part of this publication may be reproduced, stored in a retrieval system, or transmitted, in any form or by any means, electronic, mechanical, photocopying, recording, or otherwise, without the written permission of the author.

First published by Dog Ear Publishing
4011 Vincennes Rd
Indianapolis, IN 46268
www.dogearpublishing.net

dog ear
PUBLISHING

ISBN: 978-1-4575-4521-4

This book is printed on acid-free paper.

Printed in the United States of America

FOR CAROL WHO LOVED ME SO MUCH

TABLE OF CONTENTS

INTRODUCTION..1

PART 1
AMERICA HEADING FOR THE TRASH HEAP OF HISTORY 5

A SUCCESSFUL FAILURE..6
LOOK BEHIND THE CURTAIN..8
OVER THE CLIFF...10
AINO 11
WILL WE EVER LEARN 13
UNTIL WE...15
THE STRENGTH OF DIVERSITY 17
WE WANT THE ISSUE..19
TOWERS 21
DON'T BLAME OBAMA 23
ELECTION SCENARIO 2016 25
SAINTHOOD FOR TED 27
A NEW SAINT 29
IGNORANCE AND STUPIDITY 31
DISOBEDIENCE..33
PRINCIPALITIES AND POWERS 35
GORE 0; GOD 1...37
PPA 39
WAKE UP! 41
HYPHENATED AMERICANS 43
THE GOP 45
ENTERTAINMENT...47
AFTER APRIL FIRST 49
REPEAL ROE V. WADE NOW 51
IMMIGRATION PROBLEMS 53
PC GOOD SAMARITAN 55
IMMIGRATION..57
REGULATIONS...59

CLIMATE CHANGE 61
REPEAL AND IMPEACH 63
OPEN MARRIAGE 65
SHIRTSLEEVE CHRISTIANS 67
BAD TEACHER 69
WHO IS HIS TEACHER? 71
CANDY 73
STAN MUSIAL 75
ANDY THE TINTER 77
IGNORING EVIL 79
MARS 81
PYRAMIDS 83
ROSETTA STONE 85
REMEMBERING PEARL HARBOR 87
SUPERSTITION 91
OH, MR. SMITH 93
DRY CREEK INCIDENT 96
METHYLENE BLUE 98
BLACK AND WHITE 100
WHITE FOLKS DON'T COUNT 102
WE DON'T NEED A WOMAN PRESIDENT 104

PART 2
SPIRITUAL ASPECTS OF FAILURE 107

CHOICE 107
IN HIS TIME 108
CHALK 110
THE METRONOME 112
THE PUMPKIN 114
KISS 116
NO CULTURE 118
CHRISTOPHER J. BALLEW 120
LOVE OR HATE 122
IS IT SATANIC? 124
IS IT OUR TIME? 126
TREES 128

DANIEL	130
THROWN OUT OF THE TENT	132
CROSSING THE BULL PEN	134
EASIER SAID THAN DONE	136
END OF THE WORLD	138
NEAR THE END	140
HE HAS NO ARMY	142
DOES PRAYER WORK?	144
WORSE THAN EDEN	146
CONTRACEPTION	148
LOOKING FOR A KING	150
GO TO THE TOP	152
CHRISTIAN LIBERTY AND THE UNBORN	154
A TESTIMONY	156
PURGATORY	158
HOW CAN THIS BE?	160
IDOLATRY	162
PHASE CHANGE	164
TALL TALE	166
WHO IS YOUR FRIEND?	170
SECOND CHANCE	172

PART 3
ANIMAL STORIES 175

DOG STORY	176
THE DOG KNEW	178
BENNE	180
HOW LONG?	182
LOST SHEEP	184
LITTLE BUNNY	188
WHERE ARE THE DUCKS?	190

PART 4
QUO VADIS? 193

MR. MOTT..NEVER MIND	194
UP THE STAIRS	196
TUESDAYS WITH MRS. MIRANDA	198
THE VIOLIN LESSON	200
FIRST AND LAST	202
LAST CHANCE	204
SUMMARY	206

PREFACE

This book contains a number of essays that address the decline of America and the causes of our impending demise. America is racing toward the graveyard of nations and is leaderless, we have lost our moral compass, our government is corrupt to the core and we are reaping the benefits of an entitlement society. Meanwhile, we have dumbed down our education so that in many cases, high school graduates cannot fill out an unemployment form, high school graduates?

Our religious leaders have lost their way and preach more social issues than salvation. The abortuaries have killed over 55 million and counting of our unborn and continue to do so, while politicians wring their hands over political correctness.

It is the author's hope that the reader will be made aware of these nation destroying trends and will react to vote for real leaders or this nation is heading for the graveyard of nations

INTRODUCTION

If you don't know where you're going; you won't get lost..
Robert Ahlf

As we approach the end of a disastrous eight year reign of King Obama, the country is in a shambles! Political Correctness drove us to elect a president based upon ethnicity and not competence the only requirement was that "he is black and the first Black President". We should have become suspicious when this candidate was not vetted and the media, our worst enemy, covered for his incompetence and his background, consistent with lots of talk and no action.

Our country today is rapidly heading for the graveyard of history buoyed up by incompetent leadership, a congress that is completely dysfunctional and corrupt with fraud running rampant. Accountability is nowhere to be found and it suggests that we are running through the graveyard.

When I was ten years old and living in Honolulu on Auwaiolimu Street, we had an unusual situation in that our street ended into three graveyards; a Chinese Cemetery, a Korean Cemetery and a Hawaiian Cemetery. As children we tried to avoid these sites as much as possible, except when there was a Chinese funeral. After the funeral the family of the deceased would hand out little red papers containing a coin and we would get in line to obtain a coin, then climb the stone wall and go to the other side of the line to collect another coin. This was fine until we went home and our mother discovered what we had done and she ordered us to take that money to the Church Poor Box, which we did. The sad part of this is that we were on welfare and bread was four cents a loaf and we were required to give up enough money for a month's supply of bread. But, she taught us a lesson in civic responsibility that we never forgot.

While growing up we attended Blessed Sacrament Church and I was an altar boy. One evening after a service, one of the altar boys suggested that we go out to play, but he had to stop by his house first. So I accompanied him over to Nuuanu Street. What he did not tell me was that he lived with his uncle who was a caretaker of the Nuuanu Street Cemetery. It was pitch dark and we had to walk diagonally across the graveyard to reach his home. We were terrified as we passed by the tombstones until we reached the back of the cemetery where we faced a tall hibiscus hedge. From the darkness my friend disappeared through the hedge and thanked me for walking him home.

I had been tricked into walking him home, because he was afraid to walk through the cemetery alone, but now I had a problem. I had to find my way out of the graveyard in the darkness and began stumbling over tombstones until I finally reached the stone wall, climbed over and ran home. While this is enough to scare a ten year old, there are more tales from the graveyard.

We lived through the depression and were strangers to money. Since my father died when I was eight years old we lived on welfare; $50.00 a month! This was for my mother and her five children.

One of the activities we did in the evening was to gather together play games or hike up to, Puowaina Crater, called Punchbowl, an extinct Tuff volcanic cone. Since we were all poor, we would marvel at any of the rich kids in our group; rich being defined as anyone who could afford to go to a movie.

Well, one evening about twelve of us walked up Auwaiolimu Street into the Chinese graveyard, scaled the wall and walked into the crater. At a high point in the crater there was a concrete platform where the city would mount a large cloth cross during Holy Week. The Army provided search lights that would shine from a park on Emma Street and project the cross into the evening sky, visible for miles around; an awesome sight.

By the time we reached the platform it was very dark and we huddled as a group fearful of the dark. Then, the rich kid who had gone to see "The Werewolf" movie began to tell us of the horror of this movie and how at the rising of the full moon, the Werewolf would be transmogrified. By this time we were a shaking with fear when the full moon rose up out of the ocean by Diamond Head adding greatly to our panic. We quickly left the platform and headed back down Puowaina Drive, stumbling into each other and looking back to see if the Werewolf was following us. As we descended the crater my brother Paul and I began to ask assurance that the group would walk us through the graveyard

When we finally reach the stone wall of the Chinese Graveyard, we heard in the darkness, "Goodnight" and our friends disappeared leaving us alone and very afraid. So we climbed down the wall and started, in the darkness, to run for home stumbling over gravestones. Suddenly, I fell into an open grave!

To this day, I have never figured out how I escaped that grave since I must have made a leap out and ran for home!

By now the reader must be wondering what this has to do with our current situation, but this appears to be a good introduction to the fact that this once great nation, founded upon Christian values is now headed for the graveyard of nations due to our stupidity and neglect of the principles of civic responsibility and the need to protect the legacy that was left to us by our Founding Fathers. We tolerate behavior that would have been shocking just fifty years ago and accept lowering of moral and civic standards in the name of political correctness and the avoidance of being judgmental lest we offend someone.

On the national level we have no leadership, our congress has been taken over by special interests, a Justice System in shambles, our schools producing students who cannot think for themselves, our military turned into a social networking system and reckless spending leading us to the scrapheap of history. Meanwhile, the vote buying legislature continues to expand the entitlement mess completely disregarding the financial burden being placed upon future generations.

Adding to the impending chaos coming upon the world is the disregard for the spiritual events that foreshadow our demise. God has been thrown out of our schools and society. Christians are being hunted down and killed for their faith, while our leaders strive to protect certain sects over Christianity. To complete the dismal picture, add abortion, pornography, drugs, immigration and television programs that promote infidelity and abnormal behavior and we have a perfect scenario for bringing the wrath of God down upon us.

Adding to this situation the politicians have foisted upon us a colossal hoax; Global Warming. This fraudulent scheme is based upon junk science and a ploy to raise money for the United Nations through a carbon tax to reduce pollution. Junk Scientists go about citing the dangers of man- made global warming based upon a flawed notion that carbon dioxide is a pollutant. A simple solution to reducing carbon dioxide pollution is for advocates for Global Warming to hold their breath for ten minutes..this would solve many problems. This hoax followed the ozone depletion scheme where CFC's were blamed for the loss of ozone in the upper atmosphere. A group of scientists, twelve hundred, signed on to this scheme while another group, 31,487 including this author, signed a petition declaring that global warming is a hoax. The media labeled the first group Concerned Scientists while the latter were labeled Renegade Scientists. So much for the media bias!

Meanwhile the churches are not doing their job in alerting their congregations to the danger we face socially and spiritually. Many churches decry the practice of abortion, yet this topic, which should be mentioned at each prayer service, is not being pursued with the vigor that this menace requires. Meanwhile, Right to Lifers have done a good job to alert the public to this tragedy, yet they spend their capital of such frivolous items as building a coffee shop in chapels devoted to prayers intended to stop the carnage. I want to go to the Chapel to pray and not for coffee and rolls!

The essays presented in this book address the many problems cited above and hopefully the reader can glean some common sense from these tales and take appropriate action.

PART 1

AMERICA HEADING FOR THE TRASH HEAP OF HISTORY

A SUCCESSFUL FAILURE

One way of judging a person's performance is to measure the success or failure of whatever that individual accomplishes. Recently we celebrated President's Day to honor our past presidents. President's Day replaced George Washington's Birthday on February 22. Honoring President Washington who was a giant of a president, made good sense. With political correctness we now try to honor all presidents which have diminished the honor of the day set aside to honor the Father of our Country. I recall that the University of Notre Dame held this holiday in high esteem and bestowed a Patriot's Award on their selected candidate. Ronald Reagan received the award among others. Then as political correctness crept in, the award was trivialized to be more acceptable to left wing politics.

Over the years political scientists and historians tend to rate presidents. Some of those who received the honor of worst president include Martin van Buren, Jimmy Carter and the current monster in the White House. Jimmy's claim to fame was his unique ability for not making a decision. When the Iranians took over our embassy, his first step was to ask for a book on Islam so he could understand what was going on. In an amusing effort to solve the problem, Jimmy called for Herb Cohen, a noted expert on negotiations. In fact, Herb gave me an autographed copy of his book, **"You Can Negotiate Anything"**. So Herb came to the White House and they asked him how to get the hostages back. Herb told them how:

- Monday cut off medical supplies to Iran.
- Tuesday cut of all food supplies.
- Wednesday freeze all assets.
- Thursday begin bombing Iran.
- Friday the hostages come home.

The Nobel Laureates in the Carter Administration told Herb that they couldn't do that. So Herb told them that in such a case the hostages would not come home until January 21, fifteen months later. And so it was that Carter rejected Herb's solution and it took the election of Ronald Reagan to free the hostages 15 months later.

While some consider Obama the worst president, I believe that he is the most successful. This monster took one of the world's greatest countries and in five years turned it into a banana republic. With a soaring debt, a destroyed health care system, brown shirt surveillance of citizens, high unemployment, loss of respect around the world and emasculating congress and the Supreme Court, Obama has been the most successful president we ever had. He has single handedly done what no armies could do and without firing a single shot. With the assistance of a compliant media and people like the Bilderbergs and business tycoons like George Soros and Jeffrey Immelt, he must be the most successful president we ever had.

This truly makes Obama a successful failure for dumping America onto the trash heap of History!

LOOK BEHIND THE CURTAIN

***A* puppeteer** is a person who manipulates an inanimate object, such as a puppet, in real time to create the illusion of life (*Wikipedia*). For the last five years the American people have been living with one of the greatest puppet shows since the Revolutionary War. That puppet is B. Hussein Obama. In a real puppet show the puppet is made to look alive and perform to the wishes of the puppeteer. This is exactly what is happening in America today.

Imagine that this puppet has never been fully vetted regarding his educational background, where his financial support came from and just who is pulling his strings. Can you imagine someone who has gone through major universities and no one can recall being in his classes. Where are his diplomas and his law license?

A clear answer is that someone wants an agenda and Obama is driving the bus with orders from the puppeteer. Most presidents have very powerful men or women behind the curtain directing their policies, but they remain out of the spotlight. This was clear with Colonel House who played in the shadows, but made sure that President Wilson signed the Sixteenth Amendment giving us the Federal Reserve, Income Taxes, perpetual wars and the destruction of our nation. Franklin Roosevelt had his shadow controllers, Harry Hopkins, and now Obama with Valarie Jarrett.

Citizens should ponder the current situation in this country, where we are saddled with an enormous debt, high unemployment, violence in our streets, immorality, and outright lying from the highest levels of government. Today we are facing a new threat of racial warfare. The President has been very quick to use the race card whenever it is convenient and does nothing to quell the rising tensions between Whites and Blacks! (ne Trayvon Martin Case). The current act of violence against Whites now is the knock out, where young blacks prey on whites and Jews and strike them down in a game to see if they can knock their unsuspecting victim down with a single blow.

The media has responded to this awful violence with enthusiastic silence!

Since the puppet Obama is front and center, he is the target of criticism for the way the country is disintegrating. But, we need to look further to see who is behind the curtain and expose the culprits who are bent on making us a third world country. People like George Soros and his ilk have no loyalty to our Constitution and see the destruction of our nation as a gain for their evil goals.

It is interesting that the current president relies upon the lie as a major tool of deception to achieve his (and those behind the curtain) destructive goals. The lie is the principle tool of the Father of Lies, Satan, and one wonders how many of our leaders (?) have willingly or unwillingly sold their souls to the devil to achieve positions of power? Where else can one obtain the power that Obama and his puppeteers have if not from spiritual sources; all of which end in disaster when Satan comes to collect his fee.

So let us pay more attention to who is behind the curtain and see if we can pray our way out of the coming disaster being foisted on us in the form of Obamacare, higher taxes and lowering morality.

"There is nothing more frightening, than ignorance in action"
Goethe

OVER THE CLIFF

*L*ast night we witnessed our country rushing over the cliff into the graveyard of history!

Like a herd of lemmings, we rushed over the cliff of fiscal sanity only to continue on our path of destruction. Leaderless Republicans continue to cave in the face of Democrats, who would rather see the country in ruins, than lose a political opportunity to retain power. Meanwhile, the Republicans led by weaklings like John McCain, Mitch McConnell and John Boehner and other RINO republicans talked a good story but failed to take a stand. It is clear that one of the biggest fears facing the Republican Party is not to offend Democrats or the media.

To our shame last evening, it was interesting to watch the vote count as Republicans in the house caved and voted YES to please the Democrats. What was most interesting, was that in the middle of the voting, one democrat voted NO. As the vote count continued, suddenly that vote was changed so that it was a 100% vote of YES for the Democrats.

The glaring truth of this is that the House Madam, Nancy Pelosi, must have gotten to that Rep. and told her coven of prostitutes how the Democratic Party works!

Can anyone imagine that there could be not a single Democrat who has the ability to reasonably consider the damage they are doing to the country? And, how is it that the Republicans cannot unite over an important issue and stand by principle? Can it be that they are more interested in their reelection than in the good of the nation?

It is definitely clear that we need a good supply of rope in Washington! Barring that, all incumbents must be voted out in the next election.

> *"For every creative spirit, there are a thousand souls who rise up to defend the past"*
> **Maeterlinck**

AINO

Calvin Coolidge was probably the last of the American Presidents who served before the doctrines of the schemers and planners went into effect. In 1910 the insiders laid out a plan to destroy America at Jekyll Island and shortly after we had World War I and the Federal Reserve that gave us the destructive income tax.

After Coolidge we were treated to a presidency of Herbert Hoover who was blamed for causing the depression of the thirties. Then Franklin D. Roosevelt took over the wrecking ball bringing in social security and government dependency and running deficit spending. Roosevelt connived with Churchill to lure us into World War II by facilitating the attack on Pearl Harbor forcing us into another major and expensive war. (I can remember the PBY'S flying out in all directions at 5 in the morning and returning at 5 in the evening). On the morning of December 7, 1941 they were allowed to fly only to the southwest; had they done the usual flights they would have discovered the Japanese Fleet!

After Roosevelt's disastrous four terms, we continued with presidents who were taking their orders from the 'NOVUS ORDO SECLORM, see your one dollar bill, and we continued our decline. Our Education system was dumbed down so that our high school students in many cases cannot fill out an application for welfare…high school graduates? With Brown v Board of Education we threw God and our morality out of the schools then followed up with Roe v Wade that made murder the law of the land. (*Abortion spelled sideways equals murder*).

We were able to slow the train wreck down with the election of Ronald Reagan who brought some sanity back to government, but soon after his reign, we continued our march down to the trash heap of history. President Reagan had a high regard for the dignity of the Office, but this was torn down when Bill Clinton turned the Oval Office into a bawdy house. The final blow came with the stupid electorate electing the first Muslim President in our history.

This monster has no regard for America, in fact, he is an American in Name Only; (AINO) like Republicans who are RINO Republicans and vote like Democrats. This president hates America, has destroyed any semblance of patriotism, stands idly by as our brave Police Officers are being gunned down in our cities. With the latest rash of police murders, Obama has responded with **enthusiastic silence.**

WILL WE EVER LEARN?

*I*n Deuteronomy (Deut. 5:7) God tells the Israelites that "you shall not have strange gods before me! God is a jealous God and will not tolerate any other gods and the people must not worship any other God but Him. This makes good sense, since there is no other God that can compare to the one who created the universe! Departure from living under the rule of God always leads to sorrow, disappointment and in the case of the Israelites slavery and bondage (1Sam. 8:10-18). The Israelites (and we today) have a penchant to disobey God and the consequences last over many generations.

God is not one who will tolerate disobedience and for good reason. God's laws are perfect and those who follow Him prosper. Note that the Kings who followed God's laws were able to rule and give the Israelites periods of peace and prosperity. But, Satan is never far away and as soon as things are going well, he steps in to destroy whatever God favors. Kings David and Solomon are good examples of good kings (for awhile), but they soon look over the fence to see what other governments are doing and this leads to their downfall.

One of the precious gifts of God was good government based upon the Ten Commandments, while other governments engaged in idol worship and satanic practices that were the envy of the Israelites. This led the Israelites to complain that they wanted what other nations had, evil practices, because their God (King) was invisible. In addition the Israelites intermarried with other nations and that was not permitted by God's law. This diluted the strength of the government as illegal immigration does today.

A very egregious practice was idol worship which we practice widely today. (Our TV performers, sports figures and obnoxious public figures are revered in spite of their immoral behavior).

A popular form of Idol worship was to worship idols like Baal. Baal sacrifices are satanic and even human sacrifice is a part of the ritual. Even in latter times we have seen civilizations like the Mayans and South Pacific Natives worship that include human sacrifice.

In the case of Baal, the Canaanites built a large metal statue of Maluk with outstretched arms. They would then build a fire under the outstretched hands of the statue and place infants in the heated hands as a sacrifice. At least two or more babies would be sacrificed each day and the bones placed in ossuaries.

Readers would react with disgust over this terrible satanic practice and the very thought of the horror of this sacrifice is revolting. But, why should we be shocked with this practice when we in the United States alone have been busy sacrificing babies for many years now with impunity. Our abortuaries resound with the silent screams of the unborn, while we justify this carnage as legal, a woman's 'right to choose' and it is the law of the land.

We also in modern America have fallen into Idolatry and practice the same Satanic Worship that the ancient peoples did only to their doom. How can we restore this country to God's favor while we continue the practice of Abortion on Demand?

UNTIL WE...

One of the tenets of the Malthus Theory is that as an event nears its crisis point the number of events exceed the time period in an exponential increase. That is more significant events occur in a shorter period.

Consider the environment in a Petri dish in which bacteria feed on sugar and the waste product is ethanol. The population of bacteria grows exponentially, but a crisis point is reached when the bacteria are killed by their metabolic by product; ethanol.

Life in America is approaching critical mass! Within the last generation, we have thrown God out of our schools, legalized murder for innocents (abortion), declared pornography a protected right and have allowed and supported illegal immigration changing our demographics to such a point that America of sixty years ago is no longer recognizable.

Much of this demise is not accidental! In the Communist Manifesto there are nineteen goals listed designed to bring America to its knees. Some of the egregious tenets therein include dumbing down our education, mocking our national heroes, promoting a drug and pornographic culture and growing government at the expense of private industry. Groups like the Federal Reserve, zealots like George Soros and others have planned this demise for a hundred years now and their efforts are paying off.

Some of the tactics used to accomplish our demise is excessive government regulations, federal government control of education, excessive spending and high taxes.

In other areas, religious groups promote the demise of this great country by promoting misguided efforts like illegal immigration. The Catholic Church favors increased illegal immigration with the goal of flooding the country with below the border immigrants, who are largely Catholic. While this is good for the church, it is bad for the country.

Listening to the daily news is a good prescription to cause depression and anxiety. Hardly a day goes by when we see multiple shootings, suicide bombers, arrest of corrupt politicians and business leaders and so many distractions that lead one to depression. (II Tim 3: 1-7)

It is amusing to watch the response to a shooting tragedy, where we hold a memorial service and call on God to help us. Meanwhile, on the other end of town zealots are demanding that religious symbols and God be removed from our daily lives and millions are killed in our abortuaries.

What can we do?

How can we pray to God to help us in time of need when our hands are stained with the blood of innocents? Do we think that God will listen to our prayers while we continue this carnage and the campaign to get God out of our very public lives? Until we repeal Roe v Wade and Brown v Board of Education we cannot expect God to come to our aid! The answer is so simple, but like the Israelites wandering in the desert, we never learn.

God Help Us!

THE STRENGTH OF DIVERSITY

The beginning of the twentieth century spelled a foreboding for the future of the United States of America! Sinister forces were lining up to destroy the greatest nation on earth and set out on an ambitious plan to destroy America even though it would take a hundred years.

Beginning in 1910 a group of world bankers and financiers plotted our demise. In a secret mission, these thugs with the assistance of supportive members of congress went to Jekyll Island to develop what became the Sixteenth Amendment and the Federal Reserve and the Income Tax. This plot had broad implications for America.

In addition to taking over our Treasury, these demons planned to subvert America by attacking our educational system, lower the moral code, introduce drugs and pornography, destroy the family unit and involve us in perpetual warfare.

One of the villains chosen to destroy education was John Dewey who undertook to unravel the quality education we had and to dilute it to levels we see today. By lowering the educational skills of the populace, we could develop a nation of uninformed citizens who could be easily persuaded to follow the leader. The new educators set out to denigrate our national heroes, scoff at our constitution and mock the values that made our country great. The new education movement overtook the universities and the teaching colleges to indoctrinate young teachers with the new liberal education system.

One of my early goals in life was to be a high school science teacher. The closer I got to graduation, the more disillusioned I became over the education faculty who were pushing new ideas and liberal theology. When I finally received my General Secondary Certificate, I refused to go into teaching, much to the chagrin of the Education Department at San Jose State College.

Twenty years later, I found myself back in a teaching position as an Adjunct Assistant Professor of Chemistry and was overwhelmed by the permeation of liberal thought with ideas like political correctness, a lowering of the respect for authority between students and professors and the idea that diversity was a preferred mode of operation. Many liberal professors spoke highly of the need and strength that diversity brings to society and education.

"We need the strength of diversity" cried the liberals.

Imagine a business firm whose mission is to make a profit for the shareholders having a management team of diversified thought and actions. That firm would not be long in business.

Our nation is 'one nation, under God, indivisible, with liberty and justice for all'. Diversity does not give us strength that liberals preach.

Pity the students who are fed this garbage, then propagate it to the next generation.

" A nation divided against itself, cannot stand"

WE WANT THE ISSUE

One of the curses facing mankind is the penchant to kill their young. The ancients would sacrifice their young babies to the god Marduk (Bel) upon whose large bronze images outstretched hand were placed babies. The statues hands were heated to a high temperature and one can only imagine the horror of the infants screams as they were sacrificed, about two per day. The horror of this sacrifice is revolting, yet in America today, we have outperformed Marduk in our abortuaries, where 57 million and counting, have been aborted since Roe v Wade. Fortunately, we do not hear the silent screams of the dying as they are torn apart by a physician who took an oath to "do no harm". We do not call this procedure murder, because we have dumbed the population down to accept to this as choice, a woman's right to her body or a woman's health issue.

During the Clinton Administration there was much concern about developing a Health Care Plan for the country. Senator John Breaux took up the challenge and his committee developed a plan to address the issue. When he presented his plan to President Clinton, Clinton told him that he did not want a solution as presented by Senator Breaux, because Clinton wanted the issue as a political tool to fight the opposition.

In this country we have seen the rise of groups that support abortion and a profitable industry has evolved to provide this service. Groups like Planned Parenthood and other liberal groups fight hard to keep abortion alive in America.

Other groups like Right to Life have emerged to turn back the tide of destruction going on. Most churches have active groups that offer prayer services, marches and speakers who oppose the practice. While this has had an effect on the public, the practice of abortion continues.

The National Council of Catholic Bishops is a force against abortion and they provide information about this terrible plague. An interesting aspect of the

Right to Life Movement is that it is a good cash cow, as supporters donate large sums of money to inform the public and to defend the right to life. Although these efforts have had some success, the practice of abortion is alive and well.

Recently, I wrote our Bishop and suggested that the Catholic Church should take a more aggressive stand by mentioning abortion at each prayer service and direct the faithful to write to congress on the First Sunday of each month to demand a stop to this practice. Imagine the deluge of mail on Washington? This would wake congress up. The Bishop dismissed my idea out of hand and we go on our merry way.

When is the last time that you heard a sermon on the horror of abortion and the need to stop it? You do hear a lot about the building fund and other money raising efforts.

If the Bishops are not willing to take a more aggressive stand, why are the faithful supporting Right to Life. Perhaps, the Bishops, like Clinton, do not want this 'cash cow' to go away!

TOWERS

From the very beginning man has tried to achieve what God had made. After the fall, the people soon turned away from God so that God had to destroy the earth sending the flood where only Noah and his family survived. Noah was faithful to God and he and his family were saved.

Shortly thereafter the earth's population grew and one way of establishing a mark of power and a competition to be Godlike resulted in the building of the tower of Babel. The tower would be a symbol of power and greatness and demonstrate that people could build a tower to heaven and achieve equality with God (Gen. 11). God used immigration to thwart the project so that the workers did not understand the language of the workers who were brought in and the tower project failed.

Later on men began to erect large tower like structures to symbolize power and greatness. The magnificent cathedrals in Europe were excellent examples of that effort. The goal appears to reach as high into the heavens as possible. The building of these tall monuments coincides with the rise of a nation's stature and wealth since as a nation prospers there is enough wealth to show off their strength and power.

One of the tallest structures in Europe is the Cathedral Tower in Ulm, Germany. In America we began to build tall buildings to demonstrate our wealth and power. In the 1930's we built the Woolworth Building, then the Chrysler and the Empire State Buildings. These buildings towered over 1000 feet and there began a race to see who could build the tallest building. Then came the World Trade Center; two towers that stood over the Manhattan Skyline. These towers were soon to come down.

In 1954 we threw God out of our schools with the Brown v Board of Education. In 1973 America instituted legal abortion and our country began its decline into the dustbin of history. Since then we have build the most colossal tower on earth; the Baby Tower. This is the largest tower on earth made up of 55 million babies aborted in the womb. If we assume a fetus about 6 inches high and stack them on top of each other our tower would reach 27.5 million feet (5208 miles); the tallest tower on earth. What an accomplishment!

The very thought that abortion would grow in America that God has blessed since 1776 is beyond comprehension. Where are the churches? Should this not be the topic of every Sunday sermon to stop this carnage? God has taken note of this and America is on its way down and we can note that the beginning of our demise was in 1973 when we threw God out of our daily lives.

How high will our Baby Tower grow? It is up to **you**.

DON'T BLAME OBAMA

In 2008 the nation began a rapid decline into oblivion. The event that started this demise was the election of Barack Hussein Obama, an unknown propelled to the national stage with the major credential of being black. The nation had made history by electing the first black president!

Unfortunately, the euphoria surrounding his anointment lacked any vetting of his record. In fact, his records were sealed from public view, his educational background hidden and it seems that no one remembered being in any of his classes, nor were his academic grades available. As his presidency went forward the public were treated to learn of his associates that include ordained communists like Bill Ayres, Saul Alinsky and other communist sympathizers. We then learned how the media were in bed with this imposter and covered up any negatives on this president, keeping the public in the dark before it was too late. Yet, in spite of this, he was reelected. How can this be?

This event had its genesis in 1910, when a group of evil men met secretly at Jekyll Island to plot the formation of a One World Government. The biggest obstacle to this plan was the United States of America and this country had to be destroyed in order to achieve the goal. Some of the immediate effects of Jekyll Island were the Federal Reserve, Income Tax and perpetual wars to drain our treasury. To achieve these goals, the Insiders developed puppets to carry out their wicked scheme.

The role of a puppeteer is to manipulate a puppet so that the audience sees only the puppet, but not his controllers. The Insider Puppeteers always stay behind the curtain while the puppet does the dirty work.

A good example of how this works is to consider the election of Jimmy Carter, an unknown. When he was anointed by the Bilderberg Group to be president, few ever heard of him. Soon his picture was on the front cover of Time Magazine and many favorable articles written about this Naval Nuclear

Engineer. (I doubt if he could ever find the Head on a submarine). Meanwhile, through skillful manipulation, the Republican Party put up an ordained loser who assured Jimmy's election. Jimmy presided over the reduction of American Greatness, becoming the worst president ever, until the anointment of Barack Obama.

Barack Obama has succeeded in turning America into a banana republic in his six years in office and is on a mission to send us onto the trash heap of history.

While it is easy to blame Obama, the American People should pull the curtain back and find out who is driving this bus to destruction.

A good example of manipulation occurred when Ross Perot ran for President. It was a three way race and in the first primary, Perot won 37% of the vote scaring David Rockefeller and the Republican Party, so they had to destroy him. Incidentally, the Third Party trick always works to elect the anointed candidate.

So, while Obama is to blame for our demise, we should be more concerned about those Insiders behind the curtain who are really driving our bus to oblivion.

ELECTION SCENARIO 2016

The schemers and planners who are bent upon destroying our country are busily engaged in an election year circus well in advance of the election. We have two parties who present candidates; the Democratic Party and the Republican Party. The latter party is the conservative wing of the Democratic Party and there is not a nickels difference between the two parties. Their main goal is to maintain the status quo, keep blacks on the plantation and scuttle this once great country.

The media provides the entertainment and have to keep the uninformed entertained now for the next fourteen months each night on TV with stories, analyses and biased reporting. To keep the low information people entertained we have daily revelations of what Hillary Rotten Clinton has been doing with her emails. Judging from the past on insiders who flaunt our laws she will never be punished. (Remember Sandy Burglar (Burger) who stole documents from the National Archives and was never punished?).

Meanwhile, the Republican Party has rounded up a stable of candidates who are falling over each other to keep themselves in the race, such that they cannot fit on a stage large enough to accommodate them. The field is so large that they needed two separate debates to sort out winners and losers.

While most of these gutless candidates try to sugar coat critical issues, they were sandbagged by Donald Trump who spoke the truth and charged forward by identifying our most critical issue-illegal immigration. Most were stunned and could not respond to Trump's onslaught and were caught completely off guard!

This coming election is the most critical in American History and will determine if we survive as a nation or drift onto the dustbin of history.

Witness the attacks on Donald Trump by the likes of GOP insiders who include Karl Rove, and many of Trump's opponents who attack him, but cannot come up with meaningful challenges to his proposals. Instead of backing this Ronald Reagan look alike, the GOP prefers to fall on the sword and crush Trump.

Meanwhile, citizens must be alert to what can happen on the Democratic side of the picture. Should Hillary fail to obtain the nomination and other strong candidates cannot be found, our current President may decide to run for a third term. Considering the mentality of the voters, he would likely win!

One may argue that the Constitution prevents Obama for running for a third term, but Obama has already demonstrated his disdain for this document and will run anyway. He can claim that his election can be challenged in court after the election, and we are all aware how that will end.

We must pay strict attention to what is going on and support the most likely candidate Trump and pray that he can outwit the media and the naysayers.

"When small men begin to cast large shadows, it is a sure sign that the sun is setting!"

SAINTHOOD FOR TED

One of the greatest honors an individual can achieve is sainthood! People who have been elevated to this high honor have made enormous marks on civilization by their contributions. Saint Paul is one of the most revered saints in the college of saints because of his great work in rescuing Christianity in its formative years and spreading the gospel throughout the Roman Empire. His epistles are read at most every service in Catholic and other churches throughout the world and his name will be remembered forever.

In America we have had notable leaders who have reached positions of very high esteem for their contributions to the growth and well being of the country. Names like George Washington, Thomas Jefferson and Benjamin Franklin have made their mark. Other famous names like William J. Clinton, Barack Obama will also be remembered in the history books but for other reasons.

Another interesting candidate for sainthood is the late Edward Kennedy! This buffoon has left his mark on America that will not soon be forgotten. Let us examine some of the great contributions that he made on his journey through life.

He became famous when he drove his car off a bridge in Chappaquiddick leaving Mary Jo Kopechne to drown while he walked across the pond to safety. There are only three people who have ever walked on water; Jesus Christ, Peter the Apostle and Ted Kennedy.

An interesting tale about Ted was told to me by a Professor at USC who was invited to speak at a Senate luncheon. The professor flew in from Los Angeles prior to the luncheon and arrived at the lunch room prior to noon as the senators were having lunch. Unfortunately, no one was there to greet the speaker, so he stood around until Ted Kennedy motioned for him to come to his table. Finally being recognized the professor walked over to Ted who asked him for some rolls and butter. The professor informed Ted that he was the luncheon speaker. The professor was tempted to use that bit of info during his speech and looked over at Ted who was cowering during the presentation.

But, enough of his minor accomplishments!

Ted Kennedy was bent on changing America and he certainly did. In 1965 he introduced and had an Immigration Bill passed that basically opened this country up to a flood of immigrants, legal and illegal that is destroying our once great country. With his bill we now accept criminals, rapists, child molesters and drug dealers in, welcoming them as we once did to the immigrants who came from European countries.

To enforce this disastrous practice we have a liberal media who are complicit in fostering this invasion of America. The New York Times is a champion of this effort. The "Newspaper of Record" was facing bankruptcy when Carlos Slim Helu, a notorious billionaire bailed them out. Today the Times are a champion of illegal immigration. For a better understanding of the whole sorry immigration mess the reader is referred to Ann Coulter's book "Adios, America".

Unless something drastic happens, like the election of Donald Trump, America is headed for the trash heap of history and Ted Kennedy will be granted Sainthood.

ADIOS, AMERICA.

A NEW SAINT

Recently the Catholic Church had a monumental ceremony anointing two former Popes to sainthood. This was a major historical event in the history of the Church. Another milestone in the church is the situation where we have a living ex-Pope during the reign of the current Pontiff.

The church recognized its saints among believers who have had exemplary lives and did remarkable things during their lifetime. One needs to recall the work of Mother Theresa who did missionary work among the poor in India. Many of the saints become patrons of the faithful and they appear to develop specialties such as St. Jude who is the saint of the Impossible. Other saints include St. Anthony who is the one we go to when we have lost something. I remember telling a friend about my Greyhound Miki who was lost. The first thing she said was pray to St. Anthony.

The path to sainthood in the church requires careful scrutiny of the candidate's life, testimonials from those who knew the saint or had some special relationship with the saint. Then major step to canonization is beautification in which the church feels that there is enough evidence to qualify the beautified to justify advancement to sainthood. A final test is the proof that at least two miracles can be attributed to the candidate.

If one searches the history of sainthood we find that many were not the great people we venerate, but they has some real skeletons in their closets; like most people! St. Augustine, who is one of the leading Doctors of the Church, lead a very raunchy life before he received conversion through the prayers of his mother Monica. St. Paul's fame was to arrest and imprison early Christians until he received his conversion on the road to Damascus. It is interesting how God chooses His salesmen to spread the gospel choosing people like Peter, a fisherman and the rest of his disciples who were unlearned men, who at Pentecost, confounded the learned men of the Sanhedrin.

There are some who have questioned the haste in which the current Pontiff has declared sainthood for John XXIII and John Paul II, particularly the latter whose reign was tarnished with the sex scandals and subsequent aftermath. Some wonder if the current Pope may have acted in haste for political or other reasons to bring this to pass.

Pope John Paul II harbored some of the worst pedophiles or pedophile enablers such as Cardinal Law who was spirited away from U. S. prosecution and given a post in the Vatican.

I am certain many Catholics question the decision.

If it is any consolation, at least we now have a Saint for the Pedophiles; a long awaited event in Church History.

IGNORANCE AND STUPIDITY

One of the most abundant resources available to mankind is stupidity. This coupled with ignorance make up a winning combination for losing. There are so many examples of stupidity working hand in hand with ignorance that many volumes could be consumed itemizing this phenomenon!

An instant example is the current situation in America where we are heading for a terminal disaster in November, yet so many people are oblivious to the mortal danger facing the greatest country in the world.

We can look back for examples where disaster was imminent but people continued on their path to destruction. For example, the people of Sodom and Gomorrah lived a shameful life style that led to their destruction. Similarly, the people of Pompeii led an immoral life while sitting at the bottom of a major threat, Mt. Vesuvius. Mt. Vesuvius is a Strato Volcano that produces explosive eruptions that hurl pyroclastic eruptions, that roll down the mountain side at incandescent temperatures and consumes everything in its path. Imagine the people at Pompeii ignoring the threat until it was too late! On August 27, 79 they found out the hard way!

In the scriptures we are warned that "When they say peace and safety, sudden destruction overtakes them and they shall not escape" (1 Thess. 5:3).

An excellent example of this prophecy occurred in 1906 on the Island of Martinique in the Lesser Antilles. Mt. Pele`e began acting up in May 1902. There were some 40,000 people on the Island and as large clouds emerged from the volcano, the governor assured the people that Pele`e was safe, in fact, he moved with his family to reassure his confidence that all was well. The people were superstitious and believed that the Mountain would protect them. On May 8, 1906 Pele`e erupted and sent a pyroclastic ball of fire destroying the city and the ships in the harbor. One person survived, a prisoner condemned to death who was in a dungeon.

What does all this have to do with us? We are the richest nation on earth and have all the necessary requirements to participate in the events listed above, yet we ignore the danger. Our church leaders fail to recognize the evil leadership in our country and refuse to name names and to cite the danger, lest they might offend someone. Most citizens are glued to their cell phones, TV and sports to stop and reflect on our danger and plow ahead rich in ignorance and stupidity.

We have only weeks to wake up to the danger.

Will We?

DISOBEDIENCE

One of the biggest problems we humans have is the second order consequences of sin and the most awesome sin is the sin of disobedience. While easy to commit, sin's rewards are paid forever.

Consider the first sin; that of disobedience. Adam and Eve had a perfect paradise and given everything their hearts desired until they were tricked by Satan to disobey God's charge to them from abstaining from evil. Today all mankind is paying the price and will continue to do so until the end of time. Some consequences include wars, deceit, murder, perpetual unrest to name a few.

After Adam's fall God anointed some patriarchs to teach the road to a good life and later followed with prophets who tried to council the people to walk in God's way. The results are clearly illustrated in the Old Testament, where being a Prophet of God was a very risky occupation. The Jews responded by killing the prophets and took on the consequences. For example, exile to Babylon, and persecution in Egypt. Even when the Jews were returned to their homeland, they soon drifted away and fell into the trap of ignoring the Prophets. The problem with the Jews is that not only did their generation have to pay for their sins, but their children also inherited the wrath of God.

The last straw was the killing of Jesus! The Jews used Roman surrogates to dispatch Jesus since He was a great threat to the power of the ruling Priest Class, the Pharisees. Now killing the prophets is one thing, but to kill the Son of God is something else. What made matters worse, was that when Pilate asked if they wanted to kill their King they replied:
"His Blood be upon us and our children", thereby condemning their entire race to perpetual persecution, expulsion from different lands and killed by Hitler with his 'final solution' and those of his ilk.

While this is sad for Jews, the Gentiles are no better off. Consider the current state of affairs just in the United States. We too have committed the sin of disobedience by murdering the unborn and calling it choice, rampant use of drugs and making pornography legal, rampant corruption and for forth.

Remember, God is very patient, but I am certain there must be an upper limit to His patience. One can only speculate on the time we have left to straighten out our moral compass and beginning to behave as God would want us to do.

Judging from History the odds are against us.

PRINCIPALITIES AND POWERS

"For we wrestle not against flesh and blood, but against Principalities against Powers, against the Rulers of Darkness in this world, against Spiritual wickedness in High Places.
Ep.6:12

Yesterday, the United States witnessed the second coming of a fake messiah, King B. Obama with chilling weather as a fit setting to welcome the continued destruction of the United States under this tyrant.

The Insiders have planned their trap well beginning in 1910 with the planning and execution of the Federal Reserve System; removing the control of our money supply from the constitutional authority of congress and giving it to a system of private banks. Since then we have seen the results of this dreaded action. One of the major tasks of the Insiders is to dumb the nations educational system so that we have a citizenship of people who cannot think in terms of common sense, but are easily swayed with propaganda. To facilitate this, the Insiders took over the media and control it to this day. The second gross part of the plan is to involve us in perpetual war so that our treasury, people and capital, will be strained to the breaking point as seen today. (Note how we are getting involved in wars in Africa). This will provide a great stage to keep us on the road to decline and financial ruin.

It is amusing to listen to pundits like Bill O'Reilly, who are apologists for Obama, pointing out that he is an idealist and not the threat that he is to the country! Others like Ed Schulz and Chris Matthews sing the praises of the current monster in the White House.

How do we account for the situation we now face?

One answer is to look at the lack of responsibility of our citizens who allow Political Correctness, Abortion, Environmentalism and Corruption to thrive. This is easily understood because the left are experts at shouting down any common sense complaints and it is easier to remain quiet than be humiliated in public discourse.

If we reread the scripture mentioned above we see that St. Paul also warned the Ephesians about dark forces leading them astray. It is very easy to give one's soul to the Powers of Darkness in exchange for position, power and wealth. This can be done easily to weak humans.

So, we can see now that we are not just fighting corrupt politicians, but we are fighting formidable Principalities and Powers that are very comfortable in the Darkness where they can develop their evil and foist it upon their enemies.

Fortunately, we still have the 'Light of the World' to guide us through the evil day.

Let's hope the evil day is short lived!

GORE 0; GOD 1

One of the goals of tyrants is total control of their sphere of influence. People like Alexander the Great set out to conquer the world of his time and succeeded at an early age in his life. Unfortunately, he came in second to an insect bite and died before he could enjoy his conquest.

In recent times we have seen other tyrants, Hitler, Stalin, and Mao who attempt to control the world through the usual methods involving death, fear, starvation and lies to achieve world control. Jesus warned his disciples (Jn 14:30) that Satan would be taking over the world after He left. Surely, since then we have seen wars and rumors of wars to the present day.

In the early 1900's a group of world bankers including the Rothschilds, Paul Warburg and others set out to dominate the world through subterfuge and currency manipulation. They met secretly at Jekyll Island to craft the Federal Reserve legislation and eventually the Sixteenth Amendment to introduce the Income Tax, a form of slavery that is driving the American people into serfdom! They supported President Wilson's election and it has been downhill ever since; with perpetual wars to drive this monster engine to control the world.

Following this, in 1954, the Bilderberg Group was formed in Oosterbeek, Holland by world bankers and business leaders to take over the world. From these annual secret meetings comes the selections of our next president, when and where to start the next winless war and destroying governments who oppose them. Right now, Ireland is in their crosshairs, since the Irish Government does not want to follow their dictates that require the government of Ireland to follow Bilderberg directives controlling their currency and economy. Margaret Thatcher was summarily disposed when she refused to join the European Union. [Fortunately, she was not murdered as was Aldo Moro who disobeyed Bilderberg and paid with his life].*

*The True Story of the Bilderberg Group. Daniel Estulin. 2005

One of the great tactics of these One Worlders is to create fear among the uninformed. They generate fear using Ozone Depletion, Global Warming and other means to scare people into submission and ruin.

The best recent example is Al Gore and his Global Warming Hoax that has caused so much havoc to the economy on a false premise that we must control carbon dioxide or we shall perish. With many sycophants cheering this moron on we have seen a major upheaval to our economy and panic for no good reason.

People like the Bilderbergs and their agents (Al Gore) count on fear to succeed in their evil. Fortunately, God has the upper hand and has made these fools a laughing stock with the coldest weather on record to confound these liars.

Sorry Al.

PPA

During the cold war, the United States and Russia held meetings to reduce the threat of nuclear war. These meetings were big deals for the drive-by media and we witnessed people like Henry Kissinger and others who gave us détente, peaceful coexistence and other deals on which the Soviets cheated. At one of these highly publicized summits, Khrushchev was not interested in discussing the proposed agenda, but spent a lot of time discussing the book Animal Farm by George Orwell. The Soviet Leader was concerned about the publication of that book in America and wanted President Eisenhower to ban the book. What was so important about this book?

Orwell described in a cynical way the pathway to tyranny that includes the lie as a major tool in leading the public into bondage. Orwell's second book 1984 explained what the future under communism would be. In reality, we are now seeing the world as Orwell defined it in his monumental books. Under the Obama Administration we shall enjoy the evil that Orwell had predicted.

The Prince of Liars is Satan and his role in using the lie began at the beginning where he lied to Adam and Eve. Since that first lie the world has never been the same as God had ordained. Today, we live in the Kingdom of Satan where the lie is the building block of his kingdom.

Evil men have been plotting the destruction of any government that provides freedom to its subjects. The lie is a great tool to accomplish their evil way to bondage.

The destruction of the United States began about 1910 with the enactment of the Federal Reserve System, a clandestine plan forced upon our citizens that gave us the Income Tax, unjustified wars and a declining education system. Much of this was based on lies that continue to this day.

For example, repeating a lie eventually leads the uninformed to believe the lie. A perfect example is abortion; murder spelled sideways. By cloaking the word as Choice and a woman's right to choose, we can avoid the truth that abortion is indeed murder. We are now past 50 million babies murdered since we fell for the abortion lies of the left. Meanwhile, our history books report the mass murders committed by totalitarian regimes by Lenin, Stalin, Mao, Pol Pot and others. On the other hand, more and more states refuse to give a death penalty to murderers and the taxpayer must support them for years in prison.

We can turn the tables on these leftists by using the label system that they use so successfully. Instead of calling execution the Death Penalty, we should refer to dispatching criminals by calling their execution **Post Partum Abortion, PPA.** Since abortion is legal this would also make it easier to dispatch those deserving of the maximum penalty.

If abortion is legal for the innocent, let's apply PPA to the guilty.

WAKE UP

*Some for the glories of this world; and some
Sigh for The Prophet's Paradise to come;
Ah, take the cash and let the credit go,
Nor heed the rumble of a distant drum...*
Omar Khayyam

In his famous poem, The Rubaiyat, the poet warns people not to be complacent as noted in the last line of the stanza.

There are many instances in the Bible where the people are warned to keep a watchman on the tower for any oncoming enemy. Those who were alert were able to survive, the fools perished in their foolishness.

There is now hardly a day when we are awakened to another terror hit or outrage occurring around the world and heading for America. Yet our leaders appear blind to the threat and continue to ignore the impending disaster facing the world with Islamic Terrorism and its spread throughout the Middle East and Europe. So far, the ocean is keeping the hoards away from our shore, but this cannot last forever.

Our Congress is supposedly peopled with educated people, yet the amount of common sense in that body can only be observed in microscopic dimensions. How can we continue to ignore the threat, knowing the recent history of the rise of the Nazi Regime, then the Soviet Empire and now the rise of ISIS. In the late fourteen hundreds, Ferdinand and Isabella finally had enough and expelled from Spain the Moors and drove them back to North Africa.

Prior to Jesus exit from this earth, His apostles asked Jesus about the end times. Jesus gave them a great discourse (Matt. 24) and warned them to look for signs of His second coming.

If we look at the major predictions in the New Testament and the Prophesies of the Old Testament we can glean warning signs of the End Times. God's prophesies are never wrong! One of the significant prophesies states that "the gospel must be first published among all nations" (Mk.13:10). As in Jesus time, the stage was set for His first coming. The Roman Empire had a perfect system of communication so that the nascent gospel could be spread around the Mediterranean basin. Today we have worldwide communications such that it is nearly impossible that people have not heard of Jesus. Moreover, if we examine a bible timeline, we cannot help observe that we are at the end of that time line.

Where are the churches? We hear nothing from the pulpits except money raising programs and a strict adherence to the past. Many preachers abhor discussing end times or signs that are appearing with unusual frequency each day; enough to overwhelm us with the fearful events in our future.

Is anyone listening to the drum beat?

HYPHENATED AMERICANS

One of the great failures of mankind is the lack of responsibility to attend to important elements in our society. Since 1910 when the Federal Reserve was foisted on America by devious 'behind the curtain' planners America has departed from the principles laid down by the Founding Fathers. The Left has given us Political Correctness, Affirmative Action, destructive welfare programs that have drained our treasury and given us a mass of people who believe in entitlements rather than self fulfillment. Some of the results include lack of discipline in our schools, food stamp dependence, moral collapse and a culture of failure. One only needs to look at Detroit to see the damage that these programs and the single party dominance in cities that have led to bankruptcies! Meanwhile, accountability and personal responsibility are swept under the carpet.

Our universities teach the importance of the strength that diversity gives to society; while ignoring the principle of strength in 'One Nation under God', as a driving force to a stable and peaceful society. How can anyone achieve greatness using diversity as a means of developing our future?

Political correctness has lowered our standards and has made people cower for fear of job loss, personal destruction and career loss. Recently, a famous chef lost millions of dollars, her reputation smeared and had her career that she worked so hard to develop end up in the trash heap of political correctness. Her offense was to have someone reveal a word she uttered 20 years ago in a private conversation. Meanwhile, those on the left can use offensive words with impunity. I was once told by the head of the Chemistry Department that grading with a red pencil was not politically correct and that I should us a kinder color like pink or purple. Needless to say, I loaded all of my pencils with bright red lead. What is more offensive is the passiveness of those who are maligned by political correctness and simply go along with the tyranny of the minority.

One of the most egregious examples of political correctness is the use of the hyphenated American. A black student reminded me that she was a African American and I asked her from what part of Africa was she? She replied that she was born in Chicago.

What then would make her a hyphenated American?

According to the Constitution we are all created equal and that by virtue of the law, if citizens, are all Americans! I do not refer to myself as a "Swedish American" so why can't we all be Americans and support the Constitution rather than try to make one special and create a racial divide?

Our valued country is in freefall to destruction and responsible Americans must take some of the blame for not opposing the creeping incrementalism from the far left.

We have a good opportunity to turn the tide at this point, since the charlatans of the left like Jesse Jackson and Al Sharpton have come under fire by the Right and this would be an excellent opportunity to overturn their vegetable cart of hate on them. It is up to us, who are strong to carry the fight to these forces of evil.

"We are here on earth to help others....
but what are the others here for?"

THE GOP

*"For when they shall say Peace and Safety;
then sudden destruction cometh upon them"*
1 Thess. 5:3"

Reviewing the history of mankind, we can cite many great successes that have had monumental effect on nations and its people. For the American nation the passage of the United States Constitution is one significant event having worldwide impact on our own people and has touched numerous other nations.

The significance of the Constitution reflects the work of giants; of men who had great vision and strong principles and most notably, men who realized that power comes from above and without recognizing the hand of the Almighty, no nation can exist free. So far we have survived for over two hundred years as the envy of other nations who do not provide freedom to their subjects.

If we look at the trouble spots in the world, we can reduce our analysis to one simple reason; the paucity of freedom. Without freedom no nation can survive!

What is unfortunate today is that our freedom is being whittled away by forces of darkness in high places, who cannot tolerate the light of freedom. Meanwhile, the electorate slowly gives up their freedom by allowing incremental disintegration of our freedom in exchange for a promise of safety and security. St. Paul reminds us that when we think we have peace and safety, sudden destruction comes and **they shall not escape!**

As a nation we have listened to the Pied Pipers in congress and vocal liberal groups who continually extract a little of our liberty in exchange for a promised security that never materializes. Witness the TSA and the havoc they have imposed upon travelers; treating old people, children and the handicapped as criminals, while ignoring the simple solution of profiling to interrupt potential terrorist activities. The Israeli government has done this with great success.

Meanwhile, The Republican Party is dead as a dinosaur! The last election demonstrates clearly that the party has no effective leadership. They are so afraid of offending the Democrats, they cave on any significant challenge defying the wishes of the voters who sent them to Congress.

The last real leader of the party was Ronald Reagan. He had the qualities that real leaders bring to the party. He was able to work with Tip O'Neill, cut taxes and restore enthusiasm in the people not seen in many years. After Reagan it was all downhill.

We need a new party to solve the nation's ills, a party that places America First until we get back to where the Constitution intended us to be. We need to stop all Foreign Aid and involvement in Foreign Affairs that are not a benefit to America; a new party that allows no RINO Republicans and moderates, who are really democrats in disguise. We need to seek new leaders like Donald Trump, Dr. Ben Carson and Governors who have good track records as Americans.

Time is running out on America; we need new leadership.

ENTERTAINMENT

When Kingdoms begin to decay there are a number of significant events occur. Some of the causes include abortion, homosexuality, immorality, disrespect for law and order, lies told by the rulers and widespread lawlessness.

A good place to start is with the Roman Empire. After Julius Caesar, the empire was led by less qualified leaders and things began to happen. Two major signs of decay are debauchment of the currency and of the wine. In Rome's case the currency dropped from gold to silver to bronze and finally to clay. With the decay came the changes in the quality of wine. Eventually, the wine was so acidic that the acid extracted lead from the pewter drinking cups causing mental diseases. This is why Nero fiddled while Rome burned because he was insane from lead poisoning.

Another aspect of degradation is in entertainment. The Romans built large coliseums for sporting events like carriage racing which later turned into feeding Christians to the lions for entertainment. As the degradation continued the Gladiators complained that they were killing each other and there were no people in the stands; having been so hardened to violence.

We appear to be heading in the direction of Rome in that we invest so much of our capital and valued time into sports like college and pro football and are becoming hardened to the violence of these sports. Auto racing is another no brainer sport where thousands watch cars speed in circles for hours.

More frightening in our time is the entertainment industry where they continue to pull back the limits to lewdness and violence which is available to the young and impressionable. In most cases children are free to watch this garbage without parental supervision that leads to warped ideas of behavior.

I remember seeing Jimmie Durante in New York years ago and he was having fun with his routine, when someone in the audience called out, "Don't you know any dirty jokes?" Jimmie responded by telling the heckler that he would retire before he resorted to dirty jokes.

That was then, but what about now?

Look at the garbage served in our media today. TV could have been a great tool to educate the massed to paths of good citizenship, Instead we have a large group of uninformed people who waste hours watching so-called intellectual garbage and learning from the trash that the media regurgitates daily.

What is unfortunate is that we are not learning from history. I sometimes wonder why we spend so much money in our colleges and universities teaching history; yet we just don't learn from history.

Now, back to my Jerry Springer show.

AFTER APRIL FIRST

One of the great plagues facing this country is our Entitlement Program! This socialist program started in the 1950's had spread like a cancer especially among the less fortunate who consider this largess as a means of extracting more from the taxpayer and creating a culture of dependence not seen since the country began.

I can recall the politicians defending the Aid to Dependent Children Act and the spending that followed as the politicians, in their quest to buy votes expanded the program costing the taxpayers large sums of money and putting the country on the road to financial ruin.

Today the taxpayer is burdened with high taxes and forced to contribute more of their hard earned money to satisfy the lust of politicians to cater to the uninformed by passing more benefits such as cell phones, rent assistance, heating assistance, food stamps and any great scheme that the liberals can dream up to buy votes.

One of the most egregious features of Aid to Dependent Children is that the system is ripe for scamming. Young women are urged to get pregnant then head for the Welfare Office and be placed on programs for prenatal care, have their hospital bills paid for by the taxpayer and then live on the subsidies that follow. To make matters worse, simple multiplication indicates that by having more than one out of wedlock child, brings more largess and of course more dependency.

A sad reality of this nonsense is that the Black Community suffers from a 72% out of wedlock birth rate with little end in sight. Single parenting is now a mark of significance whereas in saner times, it was looked upon with scorn and shame. This situation is sadder because the single parent and the children live a life struggling against high odds of success and it is a rare case when some emerge and break the cycle of poverty that out of wedlock pregnancies provide.

Here is a solution to this nightmare. It will require courage and determination but is required if we are to save our country and culture from ruin. The government should announce that after April 1 of the year chosen, if you conceive a child out of wedlock, it is your responsibility and not that of the taxpayer! Why should the taxpayer pay for the bad behavior of those who continue to scam the system and be required to pay for the sins of the irresponsible people involved?

At every crossroads on the path that leads to the future, tradition has placed 10,000 men to guard the past.
Maurice Maeterlinck

REPEAL ROE V. WADE NOW

Abortion has been around as long as man has existed on earth. Some societies had discovered drugs as a means for aborting a fetus, while others resorted to more crude methods, many of which destroyed the person seeking the abortion (back-alley abortions).

In the latter half of the twentieth century, the moral level of people around the world began a sharp decline. Some of the reasons for this decline are the conscious plan of sinister groups of One Worlders, the scientific developments of hormonal drugs that can promote abortion and those drugs that can prevent conception. This provided women with a method for avoiding pregnancy and opened the door to wholesale disregard for moral principles of behavior. The end result was the sexual revolution, the rise of pornography and the degrading of the respect for life.

The media played a significant role in the expansion of our moral decline by presenting programs on TV and movies that pushed the envelope of moral decay to its upper limit. Then we heard the cry for abortion on demand, which culminated in the passage of Roe v Wade legislation that made abortion legal in America.

The sad result is that since the passage of this barbaric legislation more than 55 million innocents have been slaughtered and counting!

The Catholic Church and other churches have been fighting a battle against this barbarism by holding days of prayer and protests in Washington, DC on the anniversary dates of the Roe decision. In addition in many cities there are marches and prayer vigils supporting an end to abortion on demand.

What disturbs this writer is that the Catholic Church has had good opportunities to bring public pressure to bear on politicians to repeal this legislation, but with only a feeble voice. For example, where was the Catholic Church during the last two elections when pro choice candidates who are

Catholic (read Ted Kennedy, Nancy Pelosi, Joe Biden) were not publicly called out by the church and denied the sacraments? During the election cycles, not a word was heard from the pulpits exposing the current president's pro death position. As a result, 54% of Catholics voted to elect, then reelect this monster.

Antiabortion rhetoric should be spewed from the pulpits at each mass until we drive a stake into the heart of this evil.

What can we do?

Here is a suggestion. Each Sunday we should hear from the pulpit the details of the Stop Abortion Plan now! It is so simple and can be very effective.

The Bishops should have Catholics send letters to their representatives on the First Sunday of each month demanding repeal of Roe v Wade. Imagine flooding the Capital with millions of letters until the legislators either repeal this monstrosity or drown in a pile of mail.

Do the Bishops have the moral spines to do this? I doubt it.

IMMIGRATION PROBLEMS

The One Worlders who have been scheming to take over the world have many tools to accomplish their task. These plotters use a one hundred year time horizon to accomplish their evil deeds. The destruction of America began with the stealth passage of the Sixteenth Amendment that gave us the Income Tax, Perpetual War and a ruined education system to name a few targets.

A valued tool for destroying any nation is to ruin their Nationalism through uncontrolled immigration. The Romans learned the hard way when they allowed persecuted people into the Roman Empire. These immigrants who agreed to assimilate reneged on their pledge and continued with their native customs diluting the strength of the Empire.

Today in America we are witnessing, first hand, the same disaster that faced the Romans as hoards of illegal immigrants cross our porous borders with the approval of our President and congress. These immigrants break our laws and have no right to the protection of our Constitution and should be deported instantly.

Fortunately for the illegals, there are many who support the cause to the detriment of our society and the safety of our citizens. As of this writing, a Texas Border Patrol agent has been murdered by two illegals that have crossed our border four times and our Federal Government is complicit in encouraging this evil behavior.

To add to the problem we face the impact of churches that are encouraging this flood of immigrants since they would shore up the ranks of the faithful. Churches refuse to call them illegal immigrants and use the term 'undocumented immigrants' to identify these law breakers. Churches are supporting the dispersion into the United States of these immigrants and providing food and shelter encouraging more immigration.

Twenty years ago, the American Free Press reported the existence of detention camps in the Southern States and they were labeled Conspirators by the Left. The Planners think far ahead and foresaw what we are seeing today preparing these camps for what we now have.

In order to do my part in supporting the flood of immigrants I have turned to my Christian Principles and have offered to take in at least two people as a start. I have two spare bedrooms separated by a bathroom and that should accommodate two people.

The other day, through my church, I was able to contact two old ladies who agreed to see my home and decide if they would accept my invitation. (One bedroom is decorated with Paddington Bear motif and the other Precious Moments dolls). The old ladies were coming on Friday night to meet with me.

Friday night and the old ladies arrived with their suitcases. They were so impressed with the bedrooms, but soon began to argue about who would get the Paddington Bear Room. This left me with a serious problem. Should I give the Paddington Bear Room to the twenty one year old or to the nineteen year old?

Since they could not resolve the issue, they both left in a huff and this Good Samaritan got mugged!

It is getting more difficult to do the Lord's work in this day and age!

PC GOOD SAMARITAN

In the gospel of St. Luke (Lk.10:30-37) we read the remarkable story of the Good Samaritan who saved a certain stranger who was assaulted by robbers and went their way.

The tale was spun to satisfy a question to Jesus from a lawyer who asked, "Who is my neighbor?" Jesus then told a tale of a certain man who travelled from Jerusalem down to Jericho and fell in among robbers, who after stripping him and beating him, went their way leaving him half dead. Then a Priest came by and saw the victim, but passed over on the other side. Following the priest was a Levite who did the same thing. (The reason they did this was to prevent them from losing their purification by handling someone who was bleeding and might contaminate them).

The Good Samaritan had no problem with this, even though the Jews had nothing to do with the Samaritans. (It would be instructive for the reader to consult John 4: 1-36, to obtain another view of Jesus' encounter with the Samaritans). So the Good Samaritan went up to the man, bound up his wounds and took him to an inn and cared for him. The next day he gave two denarii to the innkeeper with instructions to care for the man and promised to pay any extra expense upon returning from his journey.

When Jesus asked the lawyer who was neighbor to the man who fell in with the robbers, the Lawyer could not mention the Samaritan, but referred to him as 'he who had shown mercy to the victim'.

Now, in this politically correct world we must modify this story and put it into perspective. After all, those events occurred over two thousand years ago and with all of our technology and understanding today we must change this story and point out who the real heroes are in this tale.

First we must commend the Priest, who in spite of the dramatic situation, remembered his Mosaic Law about purification and saw to it that he did not break the law. (If the ACLU reviewed this case they would surely agree with the Priest). The same would apply to the Levite who had the good sense to remember his Mosaic Law and became the next hero in the case.

The Good Samaritan, who we assume was not a physician, had no right to practice medicine in violation of many rules and should have been prosecuted.

Thank goodness we have the vision of Political Correctness.

IMMIGRATION

One of the greatest faults of our civilization is that we never learn from history. Sometimes I wonder why we spend so much capital teaching History, when we continue repeating the same mistakes of those who blundered before us.

Consider the problem of homosexuality that is rampant in our time. This is such an evil that we can trace it back to the beginning, where we learn of the fate of Sodom and Gomorrah when God became so angry at the people that he destroyed those cities (Gen. 19:24). However, this evil returns over and over to destroy the Greeks, Romans and soon our own nation.

Another evil is that of immigration or rather illegal immigration. In recent times, our educators have indoctrinated our society that diversity is our strength, whereas our Founding Fathers claimed "one nation under God" where we would all be Americans and not hyphenated Americans. The evil of illegal immigration doomed the Roman Empire when they let the barbarians come into their country and did not assimilate with the Roman culture.

Europe is now in a state of total confusion because of immigration, when they began to allow Arab immigration into Germany, France and Great Britain. These people keep their Middle Eastern culture and eventually destroy the host country. (Remember Ferdinand and Isabella in Spain who drove out the Moors at the time of Columbus discovery of America?)

The illegal immigration fostered by our government and Marxist supporters is doing the same to us. The Catholic Church supports illegal immigration to further their own goals, while the Marxists in our government are using this method to turn us into a Third World country.

While thinking about this recently, I am reminded of the story of the Tower of Babel. After the flood, the people of Shinar began to build a large ziggurat to heaven and we are told that God confused their language (Gen 11:1-9) and they could not finish the structure.

Could it be that the people of Shinar could not build this 300 foot tower without the help of other tribes and hence became the victims of immigration that wiped out the project? The people of God defied him and built the Tower. We have a similar situation in the World Trade Center. Instead of repenting after 9-11, we rebuilt our Tower of Babel, but God is waiting at the pass to tear it down again (Isa. 9:10).

Perhaps we should close down all the History Departments in our Universities; since although they teach history, they fail to teach us the lessons of History.

REGULATIONS

Ever since 1910 when the Federal Reserve Plot was being hatched at Jekyll Island, this country has been on the road down to the dust bin of history. The Federal Reserve has worked for a hundred years using creeping incrementalism to strip us of our freedom and was able to close the trap door on the ignorant with the election of the current president in 2008!

One of the major tools used to drive this bus over the cliff is the use of regulations that stifle creativity and places enormous burdens on the private sector and the citizens who have to pay for regulations, many of which defy common sense. For example when regulators found that infants were drowning in used 5 gallon paint containers a committee of government regulators solved the problem by demanding that holes be punched in the containers.

When I first joined Whirlpool Corporation, I informed the Vice President that I planned to live in Granger. He told me that was fine since they were building a new highway that would shorten my driving time. What the VP did not know was anything about butterflies! Twenty three years later, when I retired, that road was finally completed as far as Berrien Springs because the environmentalists had found a rare butterfly living near Sodus. The legal fight went on for many years and cost skyrocketed. When the road was finally completed, they found that the butterfly lived all over that area had continued to thrive.

Where is the accountability for those who held this project in limbo for so long?

Citizens should have fought the EPA early in its inception and actually the legislation should have never been given a chance to survive.

The current administration has declared war on the coal fired electric industry. Stricter rules are being promulgated to reduce emissions, while the real goal is to drive these industries out of business and replace it with liberal friendly windmills. This is utter foolishness since China and other countries do not enforce regulations and the rules hamstring our own energy base.

I would recommend that the CEO's of the coal fired electric generators, shut down their plants and not waste money on compliance. Then they could sell their assets and distribute the assets to their stake holders.

Meanwhile, electric customers could be referred to the EPA or the White House to provide their electric power.

Complex problem–Simple solution.

CLIMATE CHANGE

One of the best tools of the planners of Global Control is to put fear **into** the heart of subjects so that they will follow any mandates that leaders need to gain and maintain control!

For years now this tactic has been successful and much legislation is passed because of this. For example, the Patriot Act Legislation would have never made it through congress prior to September 11, 2011. After that carnage legislation was easily passed by the congress, much of which would never pass muster under normal conditions.

One way to put fear into people is to project catastrophic events that would destroy our civilization. Many of the regulations passed by congress and expanded by the EPA are very costly, inhibit business growth and have little real benefit. But the regulators continue to pursue this nonsense. One of the richest fields for exploitation has been related to global weather.

Beginning in the late sixties, we were threatened with a loss of the ozone layer that was blamed on methane and chlorofluorocarbons (CFC). Here was a cause célèbre` for the globalists. The culprit was refrigerants and aerosol propellants.

(The real issue was that the patents for CFC's were expiring and the chemical firms needed to develop new CFC's to extent the patent life. The EPA was complicit in pushing this effort and a Montreal Protocol was formed to address the problem. The chemical structure of the CFC was changed and a hydrogen atom replaced a fluorine atom to make the CFC less reactive to ozone. The consequence was that the new CFC could be easily dehydrohalogenated forming hydrochloric acid shortening the live of the appliance used.)

The end result was a higher cost for CFC'S and the emergence of a black market to sell the old CFC'S at a great profit. In addition, appliance costs rose to satisfy the higher price of the modified CFC'S.

Now that this issue had less fear value, the planners needed another threat and they found it in Global Warming. We were soon told of rising ocean levels, melting icecaps and decline in the population of Polar Bears. Efforts to push Global Warming were hampered by nature. Unusual cold weather, less hurricanes and other events declared Global Warming to be a **colossal hoax!** Some 2000 Scientists declared for Global Warming, while 31,487, including 9,029 Ph.D's declared GW a hoax! The media hailed the former as Concerned Scientists and the latter Renegade Scientists.

Scholars like Al Gore quickly recognized the value of pushing this hoax and have been doing it with vigor. Recently, a worldwide conference was held in Paris to attack the problem; now labeled Climate Change, since Global Warming was made foolish by nature.

Many academics have made good money obtaining research grants to study Global Warming and have provided fodder to support the myth in spite of data that denies their claims.

An interesting aside is that Einstein became interested in Global Warming and had developed an equation to describe the phenomenon. Due to his advanced age he did not publish his work. After his death, an examination of his notes at Princeton showed that he had indeed solved the equation:

$$G_w = gB/\pi$$

G_w = Global Warming Hoax

g= the Gore Constant i an imaginary number

B = Bullshit

π = a number that goes on forever

Meanwhile, the Vatican has joined forces with the United Nations to promote the myth of Climate Change and encouraging its members to follow Al Gore over the cliff of Climate Change.

REPEAL AND IMPEACH

*W*hen bad things happen people tend to look for solutions and in many cases emotions overcome common sense and the solutions reached have serious unintended consequences. A good example of this is the response in the early twentieth century to the ravages of drunkenness that destroyed many a good person, families and the society in general.

Early pioneers against drunkenness include Carrie Nation and the Anti Saloon League who worked tirelessly to pass laws that would outlaw alcohol as an item of commerce. These groups finally succeeded in passing the 18th amendment to the Constitution on January 16, 1919. This law was hailed by its supporters who would now see alcohol strictly controlled. The results were the Roaring Twenties and a robust period that followed World War I and soon ushered in a dreadful crime wave in the United States and unintended misery.

With the abolition of alcohol came government enforcement to control alcohol manufacture, the rise of a black market and a criminal element that thrived on illegal alcohol sales, sparked speakeasies, a rise in prostitution and anarchy in our big cities as the Mafia gained control of the alcohol business.

But, the intent was there and a short sighted law brought havoc in America between the years of 1920 to 1933.

Finally, people came to their senses and passed the 21st Amendment that repealed the law.

The law was ill conceived, an emotional response and no attention was paid to the second order consequences of this fiasco.

Let us move to the next century, where liberals, in an effort to gain power and control proposed laws to control health care. Despite inputs from the medical world and insurance companies and the knowledge of health care failures in other socialist countries, Hillary Clinton and her ilk pushed for health care, only to fail. But with the charismatic new president and the attitude that this first black president (actually a Muslim) and his cronies in the Democratic Party, Obama were able to fool the public and pass the Affordable Care Act. Note the lies attached to the title and to the way it was sold to the public and rushed through before anyone could read this monstrosity.

Today in late November 2013, it is obvious that the ACA a.k.a. Obamacare, is a lie, fraud and destructive as was prohibition!

Like prohibition, this law must be repealed and quickly. We must learn from history and respond responsibly. More important than repeal, we must impeach this Ordained Liar for the damage he has caused this country by destroying 1/6 of our economy, nationalized our industries and destroyed our military.

The current Congress must be voted out with no incumbents remaining and the first lesson for the new congress is:

1. REPEAL
2. IMPEACH
3. DO IT NOW-NOT LATER!

OPEN MARRAIGE

In 1910 a group of International Bankers headed by Paul Warburg secretly met at Jekyll Island to craft the Federal Reserve and the conquest of the only nation to stand in the way of One World Government. Traitors like Woodrow Wilson and members of congress made up the cabal to destroy the United States as we know it. They did not plan to use military force, but debauchery to bring about our end. The Federal Reserve instituted a progressive income tax, mechanisms to destroy our educational system and schemes to destroy the family and morality. Using our own laws, they were able to throw God out of our schools, legalize pornography as a protected free speech, drugs and abortion, while debasing our currency with fiat money.

The key to their success was creeping incrementalism whereby the time line was long (one hundred years) and those who were losing their freedom did not understand their loss until too late. One of the best ways to do this was duming down of education and demeaning the national heroes who gave our Country its greatness.

I noticed something happening during the sixties when my children would come home and tell me that George Washington and Thomas Jefferson were not what they were cracked up to be in the history books. My son told me that Jefferson had slaves and that Washington was not that great a general. In fact, George Washington was famous for retreating and that was his trump card over the British. While trapped on Long Island, he evacuated his whole army during the night to New Jersey and was able to fight another day.

I then inquired about my children's teachers and their qualifications and soon learned more of what was going on. One day my son showed me a copy of Psychology Today magazine that the teacher had assigned for required reading.

The topic was "Open Marriage" by a California Professor of Psychology who explained the requirement for successful Open Marriage and some of the pitfalls. A youngster reading this garbage could easily be convinced that the professor was right.

Where was the flaw?

I read the article and could not find the flaw until I read the CV of the Professor that read like this; "Professor Duh graduated from Chico State College and received a PhD in Psychology from USC. Professor Duh is currently driving a taxi in San Diego!)

So much for these authorities who brain wash their students and by default their parents. This can explain how High School Graduates (?) cannot read or write yet graduate leaving the future with a dead brain pool.

SHIRT SLEEVE CHRISTIANS

There is only one true church, the Church of Jesus Christ. That is, Christ is the head of the Universal Church of Christians and true Christians must recognize and accept Jesus Christ as their personal Lord and Savior. His charge to Christians **"Love God, Love Neighbor** is very simple, yet difficult to fulfill in any age.

Life can be very difficult for Christians as the Apostles found out after Christ returned to Heaven. The price for early Christians was death at the hand of the Romans or the Pharisees. St. Paul found out the hard way, as everywhere he travelled the Jews followed him and tried to unravel his mission.

Today we have many religious groups that claim Christianity as their base and many sects that have their own interpretation of scripture. In addition there has been a rise in TV Evangelists and other Evangelists like Rick Warren, Rod Parsley, Pat Robertson and Joel Osteen who pump their versions of Christianity to roaring crowds. They also benefit from the largesse of donors who support their ministries.

There are a number of issues that any true Christian must deny if they expect to be welcomed into the Kingdom of God. These include abortion, homosexuality and idol worship. These acts are an abomination to God and there is no way to argue around these issues. These three issues are nation destroyers and there are enough examples in history to verify the facts. Examples include Sodom and Gomorrah, Pompeii and Greek culture.

Today America is facing the same elements of destruction with a rise in unrest, decline in moral standards, pro abortion, pornography and acceptance of actions that were intolerable two generations ago. In fact, America is headed for the trash bin of history.

One of the very shocking aftermaths of the recent election was that over 21% of Evangelical Christians voted for Obama! Yes, 21% of Evangelical Christians voted for Obama! With little exception, the Catholic Church responded from the pulpits with enthusiastic silence!

My first thought is how anyone, who claims to be a Christian, can vote for a monster who embraces the three abominations mentioned above? In my opinion, these people are not real Christians, but Shirtsleeve Christians who when put to the test failed miserably.

Recently Christians in Oregon faced a decision to declare their Christianity as a lunatic asked if they were Christian, then proceeded to shoot those who were. This was a great demonstration of Faith and one that took courage!

So it is very easy to claim to be a Christian, but when push comes to shove, how many will stand?

BAD TEACHER

One of the most significant events in an individual's life while growing up is to encounter one or several good teachers. I am certain that any reader of this essay will agree about the importance of a good teacher. A good teacher can develop the creativity, drive and enthusiasm in their students. On the flip side, students who encounter a bad teacher can also be influenced and ever turned away from a subject of interest because of a bad teacher. In reality, good teachers are a treasure from God because of the impact they leave on a student.

When I was in High School, I met several good teachers. Mr. C. P. Klassen was my algebra teacher and also taught music, choir, and was a deeply religious man. Upon graduating he gave me a New Testament and cited Ps. 32:8 that has been a treasure to me all my life.

Another teacher who turned my life around was Mr. John Meiscke who taught U. S. History and Chemistry. As I started my junior year with a scholastic record nearing a C- he offered us a challenge, that if we studied in the manner he would propose, he guaranteed that our grades would improve. Sure enough at the end of a six week period I received B grades for the first time since fourth grade. In my senior year I received mostly A grades.

My dear wife Carol was an excellent music teacher and she touched many lives because she taught more than music; love, compassion, encouragement and success.

While I worked at Whirlpool Corporation, Dr. Larry Garber who was Head of the Chemistry Department at Indiana University South Bend and an outstanding teacher invited me to teach a class in Polymer Chemistry for upper division majors. One day he called me and told me that they needed a teacher for CHEM 100 World of Chemistry and that there would be 40 students.

Shortly after he advised me that 65 students had signed up and he apologized for the extra load.

As the semester was half over I noticed that Linda Gray was failing all of her weekly quizzes, so I summoned her to my office to see if I could determine the cause of her failure and how to improve her grade. [Ironically, Linda's father, Dr. Gray, served with me at the Army Chemical Centers Clinical Investigation Laboratory in Maryland and was a physician]

I asked Linda to show me her class notes and they were perfect, and she told me that she had hired a tutor. So I began asking her some questions:

Prof. Miranda: What do you think is the problem, Linda?"
Linda: First of all you should not call yourself Dr. since you are not a physician.
Prof. Miranda: O.K. but my diploma says otherwise.
Linda: The second reason is that you don't know how to teach and you are the worst teacher I ever had.
Prof. Miranda: Well, let's see what I can do to help you pass this course.

Shortly after the semester ended, Linda received an F in spite of my efforts. I relayed my encounter with Linda to Dr. Garber indicating that she would have to repeat the course in the summer, a course that Dr. Garber would teach. About that time Dr. Garber received the Outstanding Teacher Award at IUSB.

Later in September, I met Larry in Martins store and he told me that Linda had indeed taken CHEM 100 and flunked again. When he asked her what the problem was she said:

"You are the worst teacher I ever had!"

WHO IS HIS TEACHER?

*I*n the Book of Romans, Paul asks:"*Who hath known the mind of the Lord; and who has been his counsellor (teacher)?* (Rom. 12:34). Here, Paul is referring to the question asked by the prophet Isaiah (Isa. 40:13) in which the prophet is attempting to describe God. While Paul had Gamaliel for a teacher, we have no record of who was God's teacher. Over the recorded history of mankind there have been many notable teachers, who leave either a good or bad legacy. Teachers like Jesus, Paul, and others have given us remarkable lessons in behavior and life choices. Other Teachers, like Karl Marx and V. Lenin have left a trail of misery as their contribution to society.

One of the best teachers I have ever known is Carol Miranda, my wife of 58 years. She was a self taught piano teacher and at age 15 began teaching in her neighborhood of Atherton, California for 25 cents a lesson. She was very fond of the classics and made every effort to hear great artists at the San Francisco Opera House. She once skipped school to attend a concert by Artur Rubinstein. In fact, she got to meet him and presented him with her pencil drawing of him, which he autographed. In turn, he gave her an autographed copy of his picture.

Carol taught all of our children either piano or violin. As the children were growing up the South Bend Youth Symphony was started to encourage young people in music. Students would have to audition and if they were accepted, would play in the Symphony. This required Saturday morning practice at Indiana University South Bend from 9 am to noon. The youth symphony would also feature an outstanding artist when they won a state contest in the season's final concert. The South Bend Teachers Association members all worked their students hard to achieve high performance. Carol did not join the Association and was not well known by members of the Association.

One year our son Michael won a Gold Medal at the State Competition and was invited to play The Engulfed Cathedral by Claude Debussy. Carol and I were sitting in the audience and listened to a conversation during the performances by members of the SBTA who sat behind us. When Michael began to perform we heard the following:

SBTA: Who is this student?

SBTA: Who is his teacher; who does he study with?

SBTA: I don't know; not in our group!

When the concert ended to great applause, Carol turned around and said:

CAROL: He studies with his Mother.

SBTA: He studies with his Mother. He studies with his Mother.

CAROL: AND I AM HIS MOTHER!

CANDY

When I was growing up in Honolulu, we lived on Awaiolimu Street. This street branched off from Lusitana Street that ran down to the center of Honolulu. At the corner of this street was a small grocery store, Chun Ho Lee, operated by two Chinese gentlemen. The most impressive display in that store was the candy counter, which was at the front of the store in a glass case. Atop the glass case were large glass jars of candy and my friends Pig, Eddie Medeiros, my brother Paul and me would sit and look at these jars with a mouth watering gaze; almost hypnotic.

The candy we were lusting over was not ordinary candy! The glass jars were filled with such treasures as semoi; a salted plum with several levels of salt. There was sweet semoi which was indeed sweet and came as individual processed plums containing licorice flavoring. Also on exhibit were jars of increasingly salted semoi; the most salted was sour seed (pronounced sawa seed!). Then there were footballs, made from dried and salted olives and were shaped like footballs. Another favorite was cracked seed a crushed prune that contained the cracked prune seeds and was scooped into a paper bag. We would squeeze the sides of the bag to extrude a piece of cracked seed.

Another favorite was ginger. There were two varieties; red and white ginger. The white ginger was pretty strong, so we favored the red ginger. In addition to this was chipped red ginger served in small packages and very delicious. When you eat ginger make sure there is an adequate supply of water handy.

Finally, there was a big jar of mango seed; one of our favorites, though in the era of the great depression any of these was considered favorites. The big problem for us was financial. We lived on welfare and had no money and any one of us who could come up with a nickel was considered rich. On occasion one of us would come up with a nickel and were able to buy a bag of semoi. The ritual of purchase and consumption was like a religious high feast.

We would march up to Chun Ho Lee and the designated High Priest (the one who had the nickel) would announce that he wanted a nickel's worth of semoi. The acolytes would be wild eyed watching the clerk fill the bag wishing he would add some extra semoi. The High Priest would then offer one semoi to each of the acolytes as we savored the semoi as long as the flavor clung to the pit. The trick now was for the High Priest to be assured that he would get the lion's share of semoi, since it was his nickel.

Since we were so poor these High Holy Days did not occur too often.

After leaving Hawaii, I always made an effort to visit Chinatown in Chicago and relive the thrill of buying ginger and semoi and enjoy the memory of High Holy Days in Honolulu.

I had just returned from a business trip to Chicago and bought a good supply of red ginger. My son Beamer was visiting and we were building a wine rack. As we were assembling the rack we were also feasting on red ginger; a very addictive candy, like chocolate where you cannot stop eating after the first piece. By the end of the day our blood pressure must have reached the maximum from all the salt we ingested.

So my memory of candy is different from others; since it also reminds me of those High Holy Days in Honolulu.

STAN MUSIAL

Recently, one of the great baseball giants, Stan [Stan the Man] Musial passed away. He was an all time great in the annals of baseball, a good citizen, family man and set many records over his long career. While never a baseball fan, I did admire him for his achievements playing for the St. Louis Cardinals for seventeen years.

When I was Director of Research for the O'Brien Corporation, I used to participate in local Chamber of Commerce events and recall meeting Margaret Prickett, Mayor of Mishawaka and a great leader. During the era of Lyndon Johnson, free government money began to pour into the coffers of cities to fund projects like school bussing, affirmative action and infrastructure improvements. South Bend mayor, Lloyd Allen, accepted a significant government handout to fund the tearing down of the Michigan Avenue shopping district to make a shopping mall. This placed a severe financial burden on the merchants in South Bend, who lost a lot of money during construction of the mall. Meanwhile, the city of Mishawaka did not accept free government money and the businesses in South Bend moved to Mishawaka to form a thriving shopping magnet.

During my discussion with Mayor Prickett, I mentioned to her that I noted that she did not accept any Federal money. She told me that there were long strings attached to Federal money and she was right as Mayor Allen was to painfully learn.

The University of Notre Dame has an annual Football Banquet and I was given a ticket to attend. The speaker for this important event was Stan Musial. Stan, I believe, had only a grade school education, but he insisted that his son would go to a university. So during Stan's talk he mentioned how proud he was to have his son at Notre Dame. On Parents Day, Stan visited his son and wanted to have a father to son talk that went something like this:

STAN: How do you like school?
SON: Great!
STAN: How are you doing in spelling?
SON: I don't take spelling, Dad.
STAN: How are you doing in arithmetic?
SON: I don't take arithmetic.
STAN: How are you doing in grammar?
SON: I don't take grammar.
STAN: Then why am I spending so much money to send you to Notre Dame?

Stan Musial was a real champion!

ANDY THE TINTER

*A*fter graduation from Notre Dame, I became Director of Research for the O'Brien Corporation. The company manufactured quality paints and varnishes and was a popular brand in the industry. In addition to its house paints and marine varnishes they also produced and sold Industrial Finishes including automotive, appliance and metal decorating coatings.

A visit to any paint manufacturing plant reveals a complicated series of operations. Paint basically consists of pigment, binder, solvent and additives. The pigment provides bulk and hiding, such as titanium pigment, a very white pigment. Pigments also provide corrosion protection and color. The solvent portion provides the correct fluidity so the paint can be applied by brush, spray or roller applications. Beginning in the late 1960's the EPA began a war on solvents and removed many solvents like mineral spirits, xylene and other hydrocarbon solvents that the EPA cites as smog producers or health hazards. Additives provide protection from skinning, foam reduction and flow control as well as driers that catalyze the cross linking of vegetable oil based binders. (Pressure from the EPA has put good companies out of business a notable case was the demise of the Gilbert Spruance Company in Philadelphia. They were caught in the broad net type of legal case and destroyed. Spruance hired a disposal firm to handle paint wastes, but the firm dumped the waste improperly and Spruance was blamed.)

The last major component the vehicle or binder holds the pigment together, provides surface wetting and protection that paint provides. What is amazing is that a $100,000 automobile is protected by just a few thousandths of an inch of paint; a small fraction of the cost yet a critical requirement.

To produce paint, a standard formula is followed. The first step is to disperse the pigment in a binder which may be an acrylic or polyester polymer that is synthesized separately. The pigment is ground in a ball mill, sand mill or other type of disperser. Once the pigment is dispersed the solvent and other additives are included and the paint packaged.

Before paint is finished there is an important step called tinting to bring the paint up to specifications. Before instrumental tinting, paint makers relied on the skill of tinters who by years of experience can bring paint up to specifications. For example we made a white paint for Budweiser and it was necessary to tint it to a red shade so that when the blue paint was applied, the white appeared white.

One of our best tinters was Andy. He was a big rolly-polly guy who when not tinting used to hang around the labeling department and talk to the two women who worked there. One summer one of the ladies was on a two week vacation and Andy missed her. One morning Andy saw that she was back and snuck up behind her to surprise her. He reached around and grabbed her sleep aids (read boobs) and said, "Hi". The only problem was it was the wrong lady and Andy scurried off ten minutes ahead of the posse'.

Lucky for Andy it was before sex discrimination laws ruled or poor Andy would be looking at life through barred windows.

Andy was our best tinter!

IGNORING EVIL

One of the great failures of mankind is the lack of responsibility to attend to important elements in our society. We tend to overlook evil doings and with the introduction of political correctness we abhor criticism of bad behavior. We do not need to go far in our recent past to see egregious events occur before our eyes and shrug it off as "just politics" or "that's the way it is".

What used to be hidden is now out in the opening would have never been allowed two generations ago. Much of our trouble has come from political programs and judicial decisions that continue to erode our moral path and slowly destroys our national well being. A few examples will suffice.

When the Supreme Court threw God out of our schools and was unable to call pornography by its real name, they set the stage for the moral decline we are enjoying today.

Consider the Presidency of Bill Clinton, who from the first day brought a carload of sleeze and disrespect for the Office of the Presidency. From the beginning of his term of office, scandal was strewn all over the landscape and it was disgusting how many rose to defend his misdeeds. He trashed the dignity of the White House with the Monica Lewinsky affair and his poor choice of staff. Yet, if he were to run again the foolish voters would rush to the polls to return him to office. We as citizens have lost our moral compass and turned our back on ethics and morality.

Much of the enabling of this path to destruction has not occurred by accident. For a hundred years now evil men have plotted the gradual extinction of our Great Republic by dumbing down our education so that children don't know how to distinguish between fact and fiction. Recently, students who saw the movie "Titanic" were shocked to learn that it was a true story.

What are they teaching them in History class?

The bottom line here is that we refuse to recognize evil and out it.

Ignatius Loyola, in the 1500's had a keen insight into the source of all the trouble on earth; it is a struggle between Lucifer and God. It is that simple, yet we and especially Churches shy away from preaching this fundamental truth. Most sermons dance around the subject but rarely, if ever, confront the truth about this eternal warfare between God and Satan! Fortunately, Loyola based his Society of Jesus on this single premise and was one of the most successful of religious orders, until they too, the Jesuits were taken over by politics (Satan's agenda) and the Jesuits fell by abandoning the teachings of Loyola and went after political based objectives. Recently, Georgetown University is having Kathleen Sebelius as Commencement Speaker. The Jesuits too have lost their moral compass and prove the power of Satan to destroy anything in his path.

Unless, we as citizens wake up we may be seeing the end of our great country in November of 2012 and the citizens were asleep considering the choice of presidents that followed.

MARS

Mars is one of our most remarkable planets. Interest in Mars goes back to very early times and the Greeks and Romans referred to this red planet as a god of War. It is interesting to note that Jonathan Swift referred to Mars as having two moons, before Phobos and Deimos were discovered with the advent of the telescope.

Many science fiction movies and stories were written about Mars. One of the most egregious tales occurred in the 1930's when Orson Welles a rising star in radio wrote a radio episode in which the program was abruptly stopped and a frightened announcer reported, breathlessly, that we were being invaded by people from Mars. This caused panic among the people. In one case a police officer noted a car running down the highway at full speed until the officer was able to pull him over. When the frightened driver got out of the car, the officer asked him where he was going and he told the officer that the Martians were invading us and he was trying to get away…to where?

More and more tales arose about Mars. Giovanni Schiaperelli in 1898 published maps of Mars in which he described lines on the surface that he referred to as *canali* ; that is canals. This sparked great interest in that with canals there must be water on Mars and recent Mars observations by satellite photos indicate that the surface of Mars once contained water.

We tend to look at historical events through our own eyes using the knowledge we have and then try to impose our view to explain mysterious phenomenon. We expect that life on Mars would have to be on the surface, ignoring the fact that life can survive in the gas, liquid or solid state. For example, viruses can and do live in the air. Life on earth is in abundance as well as life in the sea and underground, like earthworms or cicadae.

So if there was intelligent life on Mars could not the inhabitants have learned of the impending loss of atmosphere due to gravity and the solar wind? They could have prepared to develop life and living under the planet surface and could still be there.

Sometimes our hubris overcomes our common sense.

PYRAMIDS

One of the most amazing monuments on earth is the pyramids. Originally, pyramids that received the most attention were the pyramids of Egypt. Archeologists have spent entire careers exploring these marvels and many heroic discoveries have been made; particularly the discovery of King Tutankhamen's tomb and gold sarcophagus by Professor Howard Carter. (Even the Three Stooges got into archeology when they sought the tomb of Root-en-toot-en). Legend has it that desecrating these tombs can cause death to the intruder. This was the case of Professor Carter who died shortly after his discovery from a mosquito bite.

After Columbus discovery of America in 1492, European explorers were startled to discover the enormous pyramids that were found in the New World; many that mimicked the pyramids of Egypt!

Scholars and engineers have pondered the problem of building these stone monsters and numerous books have been written to develop theories of their construction. Some suggest that using armies of slaves the builders would slide large stones up sand ramps to place the stones. Others have suggested that the ends of the large stones could be fitted with wheels and rolled up the ramps.

A more logical suggestion was proposed by material scientists suggesting that the stones were cast in place using forms. This is alluded to in the scriptures where slaves would coat the sides of the molds then a mixture of gravel and stone was dumped into the mold then water added to form the "concrete blocks". There is some credibility to this concept since the silt of the Nile River and the composition of the gravel containing the right mixture of metal oxides and silicates would permit this to happen. This is how the base of the Mackinac Bridge was built in Michigan.

In all of this we assume that these builders had no mechanical tools like bulldozers, cranes or back hoes; that is; no John Deere or Caterpillar equipment. I would propose another means for carrying out these tasks.

There can be two ways that the pyramids may have been built. There are scriptural references to giants roaming the earth, who were destroyed by the Flood or these monuments were built with the assistance of demons.

The Babylonian and Egyptian (as well as the Polynesian) religions were Black Religions who practiced Satanic rituals including the invocation of demons who have enormous strength and could do the bidding of their invokers.

While this is successful, the end result is always bad, since Satan never forgets to send his followers an invoice.

THE ROSETTA STONE

The Rosetta Stone was carved in 196 B.C. and was found in 1799 at the Rosetta delta of the Nile River by French engineers who were rebuilding a fort in Egypt. The officer in charge recognized the importance of the stone and turned it over to the British Museum in London. This intriguing monument brought scholars from all over to attempt to decipher the message contained therein. The document was written in Egyptian and Greek using three scripts, Greek, hieroglyphic and demotic. One of the scholars who made significant contributions to the understanding of the Rosetta Stone was Thomas Young of Young's modulus fame, whose work lead to the final solution of the puzzle. The Rosetta Stone listed the accomplishments of the Pharoah's and other religious practices for the priests.

After several hundred years, the puzzle was finally solved by Jean-Francois Champollion in 1822 who could read both Greek and Coptic. Champollion at an early age dedicated his life to study of the Rosetta Stone and declared that he would solve the mystery. (This is a good example of Psycho-cybernetics in which an individual makes a mental commitment to achieve a task and the subconscious mind develops pathways to success).

Champollion's genius gave the world a means of interpreting the hieroglyphic and opened the door to the Egypt's ancient history!

Another interesting Rosetta Stone was found in the Easter Islands where the ancients built large stone statues of figures with doglike faces and long ears and were aligned toward a direction on the island. Archeologists have found statures still fixed onto the rock beds from which they are carved indicating that the statues were carved then transported to the site for placement. A wooden plaque was found that gave the history of the early people, but the early Missionaries considered the writings as pagan and burnt the treasure. This was an enormous loss for civilization as we still don't know the origin and purpose of the statues.

Christians too have a Rosetta Stone and it is called the Bible. The bible is the mind of God written under the divine inspiration to prophets and scribes telling us of the story of creation to the end of the era when God himself will send Jesus to judge the nations and destroy evil forever.

What is frightening is that there so many ignorant people who do not spend time to delve into the treasure contained in this sacred book and to realize that we are now at the end of the Biblical Time line. Jesus told His disciples to watch and look for the signs of the end.

Today, we see the beginning of the end with so much disarray all over the earth, many of the plagues mentioned in the bible are now being visited upon us and too many fail to recognize the imminent danger facing Christians. Witness the persecutions being visited on many Christians today by Muslims and the growing threat of Islam all over the world.

Christians would do well to compare the content of the Qur'an and the Holy Bible and see for themselves who are the authors of these works.

Jesus told us to **watch** and we really need to heed His advice while we have the time.

REMEMBERING PEARL HARBOR

*T*his is a narrative of what happened at Pearl Harbor on December 7, 1941and the political situation leading up to this attack that in some ways mirrors the ignorance of people prior to a devastating life changing event.

I was born in Ewa, Oahu close to Pearl Harbor then moved to Honolulu. My father was an indigent who died when I was eight years old leaving my mother and five children on a welfare stipend of $50.00 a month during the great depression. My oldest brother, Wallance had just been hired as a machinist at Pearl Harbor and worked the night shift on December 6, 1941. (An interesting aside is that when Wally received his first paycheck, he stopped by the Social Security Office and told them that we did not need them anymore).

The world situation had become very unstable with Hitler on the move in Europe and the formation of an axis coalition with Italy and Japan. The Japanese had expanded their Imperial control over Southeast Asia where supplies of rubber and oil were needed to drive the Imperial Military Forces. The mood in Hawaii was that war was imminent as President Roosevelt and Winston Churchill were plotting to get the United States involved in the European conflict.

Meanwhile our military sent a fleet of PBY Catalina flying boats out each morning at five a.m. to sweep the skies around the Hawaiian Islands, returning to base at five p.m. On the morning of December 7, 1941 the PBY'S were not allowed to fly to the northwest where they would have spotted Admiral Nagumo's fleet. (This took the sneak out of the Sneak Attack). My older brother Paul and I used to love watching the fleet coming into Pearl Harbor. When the fleet was in the USS Saratoga and the USS Yorktown would stand off Waikiki Beach; a sight to behold!

The Japanese were getting more aggressive in their behavior to America. For example, when a Japanese ship was preparing to leave for Japan and the

Official from the Water Works presented a bill for services, the Japanese required that the official bow before the Japanese Flag before payment. My grade school, Cathedral School was next door to the Japanese Embassy and we used to watch Packard Limousines arrive to drop off diplomats and others.

Admiral Husband E. Kimmel and Lt. General Walter C. Short were military commanders, who would later be unjustly blamed for the attack.

To further our concerns about the possibility of war, the military ordered two practice drills whereby all the lights on the island were extinguished to create a blackout. It was an awesome sight to see the island darkened and the sinister implication that this exercise portends.

On December 6, 1941, my brother Paul and I went to Mokapu Point to crank traps for a Skeet Club near the Kaneohe Naval Base. We were paid a whopping $2.50 for our expertise and this was big money for us considering bread was selling for four cents a loaf. When we finished work, the members of the club offered to give us a ride as far as Kaimuki, near Diamond Head, from which we took a bus to our home on the slopes of Punchbowl (Pouwaina Crater).

The next morning, December 7, 1941, I attend church at 7 a.m. and returned home about 7:30 a.m. I changed clothes then went down to a small park where we used to gather to spend the day. As I crossed the park I heard a shell whistling overhead then exploding. This was followed by other shells so I assumed that the military were carrying out some maneuvers.

So we looked over toward Pearl Harbor and saw many airplanes diving down then rising back up. Soon clouds of black smoke were rising and we noticed that some of the planes came down but did not go back up. We watched this from 8 a.m. on.

Suddenly we heard machine gun fire and saw a Japanese airplane diving down at us about a hundred feet in the air. We could see the rising sun on the wingtips and the pilot frantically working the stick to avoid two P-40 fighter planes chasing him with their machine guns blazing. The Japanese plane was shot down near Sand Island.

About 10 a.m. the attack subsided and my brother Paul located me in the park and told me that we were at war! We quickly hurried home and wondered what would happen next. At about 10:30 a.m. Paul, my sisters Eva and Lorraine and I were standing on Lusitana Street by a stonewall when we heard a shell whistling. We jumped behind the wall and the shell exploded spraying the wall with shrapnel. About that time we saw a military vehicle pass by with a Japanese pilot who had been captured on Roosevelt Heights.

My oldest brother Wallance had worked the night shift at Pearl Harbor and was ordered to return to work. As his car drove toward Pearl Harbor they were strafed by Japanese aircraft. When he arrived at Pearl Harbor he was assigned to removing bodies from the USS Oklahoma to the machine shop floor. After a few hours, he was sent home.

[The Japanese made a serious blunder! The air commander returning to their carrier complained when Admiral Nagumo called off any further attacks, because they had not destroyed the tank farm containing millions of gallons of fuel and oil and more importantly not destroying the dry dock. The dry dock contained an enormous crane that could be seen for miles around and was instrumental in repairing the USS Yorktown that was damaged in the Coral Sea and restored to sea worthiness in forty eight hours thanks to this Japanese blunder. Had the dry dock been destroyed the Battle of Midway might have turned out differently.]

Now came the aftermath of the attack. We were told by radio that we were under Martial Law and looters would be shot! The stores were closed and the military finally ordered them open, but only one customer at a time and all transactions were cash. A curfew was imposed. A blackout was imposed. One of our neighbors had forgotten a light on and the military broke down the door and put the light out. It was eerie to see the entire island in pitch blackness.

Then we heard rumors which put the public in fear. Rumors had it that the Japanese had landed at Waimanalo. As the evening closed in we had no idea what was in store for us.

The Japanese did manage to capture one island, Nihau. The pilot got lost and crash landed on the island. He rounded up the villagers and captured the island. Shortly after he got into an argument with a Hawaiian man and shot the man in the abdomen. This angered the Hawaiian who slammed the pilot to the ground killing him. He then rowed to the island of Kauai for help.

The military set up campsites around the island. We were required to obtain tetanus shots, carry identification cards, gas masks and dug air raid shelters in every ones yard. The government issued new currency containing the word HAWAII on the bills so that if the islands were captured, the currency would be worthless.

I attended St. Louis College, a high school and it was taken over for a military hospital and our school was transferred to McKinley School where I finished and flunked out in my freshman year. The native population was in a state of confusion and despair.

Since we were on welfare, the Red Cross decided that we would be better off if we could move to California to stay with my Grandfather. So we embarked on a Sunday night from Honolulu to San Francisco arriving there on a Thursday morning in September 12, 1942. The ship was the USS Mt. Vernon a navy troop ship. My oldest brother Wallance remained behind to support the family. After he married, I took over the family and put myself and my sister through college.

My brother Wallance served in the infantry, my sister Eva joined the Woman's Army Corps, my brother Paul served on the USS Hoel DD 533 that was sunk off Samar on October 25, 1944. I served in the U. S. Army Chemical Corps working in Clinical Investigation of Nerve Gas.

AFTER THOUGHT

Uncertainty and fear was an immediate effect of the attack. The price of bread rose from 4 cents a loaf to 9 cents overnight. The future looked bleak but on reflection it was a consequence of the public electing leaders who in many cases are not real leaders, but lead the people with false promises until it is too late. We should recall the similarity of Neville Chamberlain, who after meeting with Adolph Hitler was seen waving a piece of toilet paper and announcing "Peace in our time" and compare his folly to John Kerry (who served in Vietnam) celebrating a nuclear treaty with Iran that will guarantee us "Peace in our time". Right!

We should learn from history, but apparently though they teach history in our school and universities, we ignore the lessons of history and continually fall into the trap of the free lunch. Today we are at a cross roads of a repeat of the folly of Pearl Harbor and one only need to look at the world scene to see the imminent disaster on the horizon. It is my wish that we wake up and elect a real leader next time.

SUPERSTITION

When Pearl Harbor was bombed on December 7, 1941, the people were left in a state of confusion and uncertainty. Martial Law was declared, a blackout instituted and a curfew. Citizens were equipped with gas masks and we were required to have tetanus shots. One of the directives for the people was that we dig air raid shelters in our yards in the event of any air attack.

The Hawaiian Religion is a Black Religion in that they involve satanic practices (human sacrifice) and many suspicions regarding the dead and the threat of curses when the dead are disturbed. We all lived in fear of these taboos and acted accordingly. A typical curse is that if one disturbs a Hawaiian grave, *that person will die a violent death.*

My step father John Holi Mae is a native born Hawaiian and a notable figure on the Island of Hawaii. I asked him about these curses and he did not scoff at them. In fact, he will never enter a cave where Hawaiians are buried or a heau (a stone lined rectangle where human sacrifice was done for fear of his life)

In January 1942, we began digging air raid shelters. My good friend Eddie Medeiros lived on Lusitana Street and my brother Paul and I went over to help Eddie, Johnny and Walter dig their shelter. In the neighbors yard Stacy Marks and Willie Olivera were busy digging a shelter in their yard. After digging a large rectangle we were startled to find a piece of chalk in the dirt. As we dug further we uncovered a complete skeleton! Meanwhile, Stacy and Willie discovered a skeleton in their shelter with a necklace around its neck.

They began to throw the necklace beads at us who in turn threw bones back at them. At noon, Paul and I went home for lunch and showed my mother the beads. She immediately ordered us to go back, pick up the bones and bury them and pray over them. We told Eddie and Stacy that and they laughed at us. Paul and I dug a hole by a large mango tree and prayed over the bones. I was amazed at the attitude of Stacy, Willie, Johnny and Walter concerning this great superstition even though we warned them about the Curse.

Sometime later, Stacy joined the navy and he was in the brig of a ship when the ship was sunk. Willie Olivera was flying in a private plane and was never heard from again. Several years later Johnny was riding on a motorcycle when the driver lost control and slammed into a telephone pole, killing Johnny. Walter became a jockey and moved to California when he stopped by to help a lady stuck on the railroad tracks and was killed when the train overtook them.

My brother Paul enlisted in the Navy and was serving on the USS Hoel, DD533, which was sunk off Samar in a battle with Japanese Battleships. He was trapped inside the burning ship, but was able to bend the dogs on a hatch cover and escape. He was the last man off the doomed ship.

So many religions are based upon satanic tenets, and doom their followers to sad lives. Witness the people of Haiti who have never gotten anywhere with their beliefs in Voodoo and satanic rites. This is why the First Commandment is such an important one for Christians.

It would be a good idea to read it every day and act accordingly.

OH, MR. SMITH

When I started attending San Jose State College, World War II had recently ended and many GI's returned from the war and attended college using the benefit of the GI Bill of Rights that paid their tuition. Many of these veterans were more mature and serious about their studies and many believed that engineering was a ticket to the future. In fact, many were later hired by automotive and aircraft manufacturers. As a result, I met a number of ex GI's who became lasting friends; Frank Passantino, who we called the FBI (Full Blooded Italian), Matt. Krumpotic, Tom Lauret and Don Mertens.

I used to work as a projectionist at the Sunnyvale Theater and on many evenings, Tom, Matt and the FBI would come over after the box office closed and watched the end of the movie. The doorman knew they were my friends and let them in. After the movie we would adjourn to a coffee shop and work on world problems; discussing everything from politics, college and girls. Tom used to rib me about how many girl friends I had (zero), since I worked all the time and had no time for social life. Then, he would tell me about his two girl friends and how he had a working balancing act to make sure they never crossed paths.

One day we hired a new ticket office girl, Lee, and as we were leaving the theater, Tom asked me who that was and I told him I did not know, because she was a new hire.

As we were drinking coffee all Tom could talk about was the new ticket girl. So I bet him a quarter that I could get a date with her before he could. (This was big money and I had to win). So a few nights later I asked Lee if I could give her a ride home and she accepted. So after closing the theater we walked over to the coffee shop. Soon Tom came rushing in and barged into our chatter, forcing me to introduce him. He then took over the conversation and made me quite insignificant. The next Sunday I took her out to play miniature golf and thus won my bet.

Lee was a strict Mormon and did not go for any nonsense as I soon learned.

Sometime later, Tom had a man-to-man talk with me, since I had been taking Lee home a lot and wanted to know if anything was going on. I told him that it was nothing to talk about. After coffee I just drove to an apricot orchard and we got into the back seat and got undressed…no big deal.

"Yeaaaaaaah?" was his reply.

So next Friday afternoon, at school Tom told me that he wasn't coming by the theater because he had a date.

"With Lee", I asked. "No, you don't know this girl", said Tom.

That Friday night as the FBI, Matt and I were drinking coffee, the door of the Café burst open and an enraged Tom rushed in and grabbed me by my shirt and cussed me out. Then he began to tell us his story.

He had indeed gotten a date with Lee for seven o'clock. He then went to Armanini's drug store and was met by Mrs. Armanani who asked Tom about his mother and began a conversation. At the end of her conversation she asked what Tom needed and he told her he wanted a pack of gum. He then rushed over to Swanson's Drug store and met Mrs. Swanson who started a long conversation and Tom bought another pack of gum.

Time was not on Tom's side, but he made a wild drive from Sunnyvale to San Jose where he was certain that he would not be recognized. So he found his way to a large Walgreen's Drug Store and made his way toward the Pharmacist. As he reached the Pharmacist, a woman cut him off so Tom walked over to the other end of the busy drugstore where a young lady asked him if she could help him.

Tom leaned over the counter and quietly whispered to her, "Do you have any condoms?"

The young lady shouted "Oh, Mr. Smith, do we have any **CONDOMS?**"

The Pharmacist came running over to Tom and the crowd in the drugstore began laughing at Tom.

He rushed to his 1938 Dodge sedan and raced back to Sunnyvale to pick Lee up. When he started some extracurricular activity with her she really put him in his place. I guess I had set him up.

I wonder if he went back to get a refund for the gum he bought?

I never did collect on my bet!

"He who gets his fingers in the jelly, winds up with his ass in a jam"

THE DRY CREEK INCIDENT

In 1942 I lived in Campbell, California. This was a small agricultural town surrounded by fruit orchards. The Southern Pacific Railroad passed through town on its way to Los Gatos. There were two major industries there; the Drew Cannery and Hyde's Dehydrator. During the summer many of the high school students including me were hired during the packaging season. Next to the railroad tracks was Martin's Blacksmith Shop owned by Thomas Martin who invented the Martin Ridger. The Martin Ridger made possible the plowing of orchards into ridges that were needed to permit irrigation. Mac Martin and his brother Murray worked at the Shop.

Most of the area around Campbell was rural and there were a few places that provided alternative activities for me and my friends. One place was the Los Gatos Creek where they operated a gravel pit and Bob Garcia aka Rotten Rodney, used to take us on suicide rides at night up and down the truck paths in his Model A Ford. What was so frightening was that there were loading tunnels for gravel trucks and Bob would roar down the trails through the tunnels. One night Bob, Merrill Grim, Frank Smith and I were on a suicide tour running up and down the creek bed. The next day I walked through the area and noted that some of the tunnels were closed. We could have run into one of these for a final car ride.

Since it was war time, there was gas rationing and we could only get a small allotment of gasoline. So the trick was to pour a little gas into the Model A, start it and fill the rest of the tank with kerosene. The car ran alright, with a minor after effect; a large cloud of white smoke, from the unburnt kerosene, that also permeated our clothes. One night we were riding up Willow Creek road and came to a stop sign. Bob turned the choke to the closed position and revved the engine producing a smoke screen that would rival a navy destroyer.

Unfortunately, there was a city bus behind us and when the light changed there was the bus fully clothed in smoke.

Another important site was Dry Creek Road. This road was paved along a dry creek bed and it was a favorite place for people to practice social functions. One of my friends George Flagel had a Model A sedan and we used to ride around town wasting time. I worked as an electrician at Drew's Cannery so I wired Georges car with three auto headlights and we were ready for Dry Creek. We drove down at night; George, Merrill Grim, Frank Smith and me. We found two social engineers parked along the road so George turned off the lights and crept close to the participants and we turned our light on, and then promptly sped off ruining someone's night.

During the mid thirties, GM developed "Knee Action" a type of shock absorber that made for smooth riding. Mac Martins dad had one but as time went on the absorbers failed and when the car hit a bump, the car would buck up and down making it difficult to drive. One night Mac, Merrill Grim, Frutie, George Flagel and me were trolling Dry Creek. We saw a parked car, snuck up on it and shook the car, then jumped into Mac's car and roared off. Since that was fun we turned around for an encore when the other party was waiting for us with a crowbar. We all ran for Mac's car and as Mac sped off the car was bucking like a bronco and we barely made it to safety. Dry Creek anyone?

METHYLENE BLUE

Methylene blue is a heterocyclic aromatic chemical compound that has many uses in biology and chemistry. Methylene blue should not be confused with methyl blue or violets used as pH indicators. It is used in treating urinary infections and causes a change in color of urine.

On September 5, 1953, I was inducted into the U.S. Army and sent to Fort Ord, near Monterey California for basic training. The transition to military service is quite a shock and demanded a complete outlook change for the poor recruit. Our group was housed in a two story barracks building and we had double- bunks to accommodate the inmates.

I soon found myself mixed in with a wide diversity of characters; some good, but many quite obnoxious. One character who stood out was a fellow named Mitchell. He bunked on the bed above mine and was soon doomed to a short career in the army. We stored our rifles, the M1 Garand, in racks in the foyer of the barracks and the drill sergeant was very strict about the control of these firearms. One day, we were sent out to the firing range to shoot targets. We were handed ammunition and advised to keep our weapons pointed down range at all times. Leave it to Mitch, he started to walk around pointing his weapon as he pleased; much to the consternation of the drill sergeant and the fellow recruits. After practice we were required to turn in our bullets. When we returned to the barracks, Mitch called me over and reached into his jacket pocket and showed me a handful of bullets that he had kept. I did not sleep well that night. Soon after this incident, Mitch was caught stealing and was awarded a Dishonorable Discharge.

Another unpleasant guy was a soldier named Modini. He had no regard for his fellow soldiers and was quite obnoxious. One day on a weekend pass I returned to Campbell and told my friend Kent Clark about Modini and wondered how I could fix his wagon. Kent's father owned Clark's Drug

Store so Kent gave me a small bottle of Methylene Blue powder and told me how to use it.

So I returned to the barracks and went on with my training trying to avoid the obnoxious Modini. Finally I had it so I bought a Mister Goodbar® candy and sprinkled some Methylene Blue on the candy and put it on his bunk. Modini was doing KP duty that night and came back near midnight spotting the bar on his bunk. So he turns on all the light and shouts, "Hey! Who gave me the candy?"

The next morning Modini went to the latrine and was heard screaming. When we got to him he told everyone that his urine turned green. So they came to me, knowing that I was a chemist for advice. I suggested the worse, venereal disease. This scared the wits out of Modini and for the rest of the day, every time he went to the latrine he was followed by a cadre of soldiers as they traced the fading of the green color with time.

Luckily, Basic Training lasted only twelve weeks.

BLACK AND WHITE

There are many ways to describe the differences between these two states. In allegorical terms we think of black in terms of darkness, dirty, evil, sinister or demonic. White is considered as clean, bright, pure and more benign terms than black. From the view of the physicist, white is a condition where all waves of the electromagnetic spectrum are reflected, while with black all wavelengths are absorbed. Another way of looking at it is that white tends to give back, while black tends to receive only.

Some of the connotations reflected in the black region include gloom and doom. In a funeral situation where gloom and sadness exists, we use black clothing and wreaths to signify mourning. Black also connotes evil. The devil is portrayed as evil, black and dark. Art work depicting the devil shows him in dark (black) array and quite terrifying. I can remember my mother telling us of the Black Man, the Devil, to remind us to be good. In the scriptures we are told of the 'people who sat in darkness have seen a great light' (Matt. 4:16); a contrast between dark and light.

In the Muslim world, black seems to be the choice in garb and religious symbolism. The Kabah (or Kabaah) which means square is the holiest place in the Muslim world. The Kabah is draped in black. People of the Levant wear black clothing, hair covering, uniforms and fly black flags.

The flip side of black I white. White is taught of purity, clean (the saints washing their robes in the Blood of the Lamb, Rev7:14), the use of white in marriage ceremonies to reflect cleanliness and purity, and the complete opposite of black.

A number of examples of the importance of white can be found in scripture. At the resurrection of Jesus, He is described as having clothes as white as snow and bright Matt.(28:3) and the angel who confronted Mary Magdalene were dressed in white. When Peter and John raced to the tomb, they too saw angels in white garments. At the Ascension of Jesus, there appeared two angels dressed in white robes asking the apostles and saints, "Why do you look up to Heaven?" (Acts 1:10,11).

In view of the above, the question may arise that if white if the chosen garments of the angels, why do the clergy dress in black? Notice the Rabbi's, Christian clergy, nuns and other religious figures choose black. Wouldn't you think that those who are seeking the Lord and His Kingdom would try to reflect on the apparel of the angels?

Why then are they not clothed in white?

WHITE FOLKS DON'T COUNT

The tragic death of Kate Steinle in San Francisco at the hands of an illegal immigrant who had been deported five times has cast a dark shadow over this country and more importantly over the current occupant of the White House.

San Francisco is one of the many Sanctuary Cities in America that provides protection for illegal immigrants and in many cases prevents them from being deported, turned over to ICE or jailed. The Politically Correct crowd favors this kind of America over the rule of law. In addition, the Democratic Party and cowardly RINO Republicans champion the rights of illegal immigrants over those of American citizens for political purposes.

Over the past year, we have experienced a number of killings of black men at the hands of the police with the expected results of riots and accusations of "Police Brutality" fanned by ordained agitators like the Rev. Al Sharpton and others in which the Police become the target of attacks, followed by rioting and looting in the streets as the PC city leaders urge the police to stand down. The sight of police standing by as looters destroy businesses is repulsive and totally unacceptable in our society.

To make matters worse, the President sends members of his staff to attend funeral services for these thugs followed by the FBI. Then investigations are initiated to determine if civil rights have been violated or hate crimes committed by the police becomes the norm.

The President has no problem sending his staff and even himself to these tragic events, yet in the face of a most heinous crime, the senseless killing of Kate Steinle, the President responded with **enthusiastic silence.**

Clearly, this President does not represent the American people and his actions turning America into a banana republic is blatantly obvious even to the uninformed. If anything, he is an ordained racist!

With the current election frenzy now going on in the country, we need to never allow the election of another fake president and elect an individual who is pro American and not one whose ideology overcomes the rule of law. **"When small men begin to cast large shadows, it is a sure sign that the sun is setting"**

WE DON'T NEED A WOMAN PRESIDENT

One of the problems with our current society is political correctness!
The pc crowd wants everyone to be equal, but they do allow for some to be more equal than others. An example of this nonsense is the drive to change long held traditions to satisfy their agenda.
We are aware of many examples of the foolishness of political correctness in our daily lives and listing a few would illustrate the point. Take for example of our athletic teams, who for years have had well ingrained names and the fans relate to them over the years. Now the pc crowd has been offended by the Redskins, the Washington Football Team. They use any flimsy excuse to justify their attacks on tradition and using legal means shut down many critics, who just refuse to spend money defending their own stand.

Another tactic is to develop guidelines for social behavior and then vote for people, not on the basis of their qualifications, but on some requirement such as ethnicity or gender. A good example of the folly of this thought is to look at many of our cities that have been destroyed because of the need to fulfill a mythical requirement, "we need a black mayor', or some such nonsense. In cities like Benton Harbor and Detroit Michigan, it is almost against the law not to have a black mayor, yet many have failed miserably due to their incompetence. In most cases these mayors all serve two terms; one in office and one in prison. There are so many very competent black citizens who could do the job, yet these talented individuals are often ignored and even pilloried.

Perhaps the best example of the folly of voting someone into office because of color is the current monster who now occupies the White House. In their zeal to push the idea of a First Black President, the media and the pc crowd plunged headlong over the cliff to elect B.H. Obama. None in the media even did any vetting of this newcomer or bothered to examine his birthplace or college records.

Who promoted him to run for President?

Who bankrolled his education?

What was the nature of his writings and philosophy?

None of this was brought forth and those who dared question the 'Messiah' were labeled conspiracy theorists or racist; that shut them up quickly!

Now we witness the folly of voting for someone to satisfy a dreamed up need such as 'we need a black president'. What we needed was an American first, then a very competent individual. The rest takes care of itself.

Not learning from our folly, we are now beating the drums for a woman president.

HERE WE GO AGAIN!

The most frightening part of that is Hillary Rotten Clinton. There are so many competent and successful women in society today who could fill this critical need.

But, we don't need a woman in the White House, we need a good American, who exhibits patriotism, common sense and strength like Margaret Thatcher.

Elect a good American President; if she happens to be a woman; GREAT!

PART 2

SPIRITUAL ASPECTS OF FAILURE

CHOICE

Ever since 1910 when the Federal Reserve Plot was being hatched at Jekyll Island, this country has been on the road down to the dust bin of history. The Federal Reserve has worked for a hundred years using creeping incrementalism to strip us of our freedom and was able to close the trap door on the ignorant with the election of the current president in 2008!

One of the major tools used to drive this bus over the cliff is the lie. We have been lied to in so many areas; social security, pornography as a protected right and abortion, when Roe v Wade was passed and approved by the Supreme Court. To sell this abominable procedure, the elitists had to lie by using words such as choice to describe the murder of the unborn.

To facilitate the lie we also use words like Woman's Health Rights or send emissaries about to proclaim that choice is acceptable, while hiding the true meaning of abortion. A good example was when Notre Dame University invited Mario the Pious (Gov. Mario Cuomo) to speak at Stephan Center. He loudly proclaimed that Capital Punishment is murder, but abortion is *choice*. The student body leaped to their feet to applaud this monstrosity spoken by Mario the Pious.

So much for Notre Dame's Catholic legacy!

A problem with abortion is the Catholic Church's stand on birth control. Using the "Sin of Onan" as a base (Gen 38: 8-10), the church condemns all forms of birth control; regardless of the ability of parents to support large families. One value of large families is the growth of the Catholic Church (a tactic used by Muslims) to overcome a society with their own kind. The same goes for the Catholic Church support of illegal immigration! In the case of abortion the act is murder, despite Mario the Pius, since a living soul is killed, while contraception has no living entity as a consequence. The

Church stand that each sexual encounter is for procreation is nonsense! Could this explain why so many Catholics disobey the church and practice contraception?

Until the Church comes to grips with the issue of contraception/abortion in a common sense approach, we will continue on our path to destruction as a nation. We cannot go on murdering millions in the womb and not expect God to notice. And, where is the church when Catholic politicians, like Nancy Pelosi, pollute the Catholic Faith with impunity?

IN HIS TIME

*A*dear friend of mine asked me to pray for a need that had gone unanswered for a long time and I assured her that I would indeed pray for her.

St. Paul tell us to pray always (1 Thess. 5:17) and for many good reasons. Jesus also commanded us to pray and gave us the ultimate prayer in The Lord's Prayer. This important prayer is recited millions of times a day, but I wonder how many really concentrate on the meaning in each word?

A great truth is that God answers all prayers! Now God may say "NO" and that too is an answer to prayer since God is aware of the consequences of answered prayer that may or may not be beneficial to the supplicant.

When I worked at Whirlpool, we had a Bible Group that I headed and a Prayer Group that Dr. Don Knoop operated. The Bible Group was fairly large and well attended and we met at noon on Wednesday. The Prayer Group was held in Don's office and attended by up to six or seven.

After opening with a prayer, Don would ask each of us what we needed that particular day or period and he would list the need and date the request. We would then each individually address the daily needs list and any other needs for which we were praying. Our prayer requests could range from some small item to a significant life changing need. Several examples will suffice.

I had been invited by the Editor of Industrial and Engineering Chemistry to write a Guest Editorial and I had no idea what to do…so we entered the request and dated the request. Several days later on my long drive home the entire editorial came to my mind and it was published. One day our Mathematician brought a serious problem to us. He was having a great difficulty obtaining a mortgage so we all prayed for Dr. Semercian. About two in the afternoon, Mike called me and told me that his mortgage went through. We developed a long record of prayers answered.

Carol taught piano and refused to teach on Sunday. Five years ago a Korean student's mother from Sturgis asked Carol to teach her daughter but the only day they could come was on Sunday since they came to Osceola to attend their Christian Church. Carol took the student who eventually won a first prize at the Stickley Piano Competition at Notre Dame. The mother told Carol that her husband needed a Green Card and could not get one. So Carol and I began praying for the Green Card each night for four years and we wondered if our prayers would ever be answered.

The Sunday after Carol died the mother and daughters brought me some flowers and told me, excitedly, that they received their Green Card!

Yes, Monica, God does indeed answer prayer in His Time and God Bless You.

CHALK

One of the great concerns of elderly couples is the thought of losing one or the other. In my case we always assumed that I would die first since I was older than Carol. Fortunately, she died first. In her case she was suffering from terminal follicular thyroid cancer and had I died, she would have been helpless to care for herself. (God always seems to have the correct solution to our problems).

In other cases the one left behind wonders why they have not been taken and sometimes propose reasons why they are left behind. Recently, I spoke with my good neighbor Norma Bietler who was dying of several complications. I had suggested to her that when she reaches the other side that she would look up Carol and tell her to come and get me. Norma in turn told me that the first thing she was going to do was to look up her late husband Ed and give him a piece of her mind for leaving her so early.

Many of my friends who are widowers have expressed concerns of being left behind and wonder why this is. Of course we cannot understand God's plans for us and what the situation is on the other side. Could there be a problem of overcrowding or a lack of angels to carry out background checks to see just who should be admitted to the Kingdom?

The other evening I was talking with my brother Paul about this situation. His wife died many years ago and he spent some time with his Rosa who enjoyed traveling and living the rest of their days. Rosa was suddenly taken away and that left him alone. He was lamenting that he was very lonely and wondering why he was still here. I promised to look into the problem for him having been a scientist for over forty years.

In studying the procedure for entering the Eternal Kingdom, I learned of the complicated process a soul must undergo to reach the other side and here was the crux of the problem; a supply problem! Upon reaching the Golden

Gate the soul is required to ring the bell and is given a piece of chalk, then sent back to the bottom of the stairs with orders to write each sin on a succeeding step until they reached the Heavenly Gate.

With all the terrorism and war and disasters going on in the world there have been a flood of souls being processed for entry and they have exhausted the supply of chalk in Heaven. Attempts to bring the inventory of chalk up to normal had been hindered because a number of liberal politicians had accidentally been admitted to Heaven and put in charge of inventory!

So this is why Paul, you have not been called for and I have been working on an Earthly solution.

Here is my suggestion, Paul. When you go up the flume, be sure that your children place a box of chalk or better yet two into your casket, so that you will have enough chalk to write all of your sins down. And don't forget the time you tried to blow up Agulia's mail box on Halloween and all the grief you gave Brother Leo in fifth grade.

THE METRONOME

When Carol was ten years old, her father bought her a Knabe parlor grand piano from Sherman-Clay in San Francisco. This piano was built in 1910 and was fitted with a player attachment and used in a World's Fair to advertise the Knabe name. The player was removed and the piano sold to Sherman-Clay. Carol cherished this instrument and rarely let her students play it, only special students got to play it as well as Dr. Robert Rhein, a Professor of Music at Bethel College.

Many years later her piano tuner informed Carol that he was rebuilding a piano. It was a Sohmer built in 1895, very ornate, which was to be painted pink and sold to a local bar in South Bend. Mr. Buckles decided that the Sohmer would be better suited for her studio, so we purchased it. This was the piano taught on and many students have spent hours playing on this beautiful instrument.

Thirty years ago, Carol sent both pianos to Cincinnati to be completely restrung and refinished to their original beauty.

When we moved to our present home in 1959, Carol's Knabe was in storage in Menlo Park, California so I arranged for the piano to be shipped here and we placed it in our small dining room where Carol resumed her teaching career. Her first student was Ray Bennett, a neighbor. Slowly word spread about her teaching and she began acquiring students including our own children.

One day after Carol died the door bell rang and it was Ray Bennett who stopped by to offer his condolences and to talk about his experiences studying piano with Carol. He sorely missed her, as I do, and went to the studio to play the piano for her.

Since Carol's pianos are so old, her new piano tuner recommended that she install humidifiers under the units to help keep the instruments in tune. To maintain the humidifier, we are required each month, to add a water solution containing an antifouling additive. Carol was very concerned that I follow the procedure each month. There are warning lights to remind us of the need to refill the water tank.

Last Sunday I was watering her orchids and noticed that the lights were flashing. I bought some distilled water, made up the solutions and proceeded to fill the tank on the Sohmer when the Metronome went off, ticking very loudly! I tried to figure out where the sound was coming from until I realized that Carol was watching that I did this right.

The metronome stopped after I reminded her that I had things under control.

Thank you, Carol.

THE PUMPKIN

Carol and I had a fifty eight year love affair that ended on October 5, 2011. We had so many good experiences that made our marriage a special treasure. She was one of the best music teachers in the area and spread her love and caring to them and their parents. In addition to her love of music and teaching, was her love for her garden. She was so devoted to the garden and spent a great deal of her life weeding, mowing, trimming and all the work needed to take care of God's Garden as she called her garden.

One of the memorable aspects about Carol was her love for small surprises. When I went shopping, I would always try to pick up something to surprise her and it was always very much appreciated. Sometimes we would play a game. I would buy her something then leave notes around the house to have her trace the surprise..Carol always liked that.

Another thing I used to do was hide presents under her pillow and what was so much fun was that she was so busy living her life that she sometimes overlooked the obvious. To wit, I would hide a box of pecan turtles under her pillow and she would get into bed, we would say our prayers, then she would complain that her pillow was uncomfortable. That was when she would reach under the pillow and find her surprise.

Sometimes, my surprise would go unnoticed for several days or longer. I remember I bought her a beautiful Teaball Viburnum and planted it near the swimming pool. She did not find it until several days later.

Perhaps the funniest event was when I bought her a large nutcracker for Christmas as she had over 165 nutcrackers that she placed around the kitchen and family room during the Christmas Season. Her special nutcracker that remains up all year is one given to her by Tom Weinberg, a Naval Academy Nutcracker and a Glass Cello that Donna Kash gave her.

I took the nutcracker box and set it behind her pillow. This box was so tall that it couldn't be hidden behind the pillows, so I just placed it there. Well, you guessed it; she got ready for bed and never noticed it; it was so obvious! Finally, she could not get comfortable and realized the source of her discomfort.

The most remarkable aspect of Carol and her caring was that she shared the same enthusiasm for anything I ever gave her.

For her Seventy Fifth Birthday, Donna set up a party for us at our home. I gave her a $2000 watch and she was overjoyed since she always wanted a nice watch. A few weeks before she died, I went to Martin's and found a $0.89 mini pumpkin and gave it to her. The reception I received for the pumpkin was as great as was that for the watch.

She loved little surprises and I loved her.

KISS

Animals communicate in a variety of ways. For example dogs whine or bark, birds produce a song to ward off territorial intruders and other creatures communicate through chemical means i. e. pheromones. Pheromones are chemicals that induce physiological responses. When a honey bee stings an intruder they emit an attack pheromone that triggers other bees to attack.

People communicate by a number of ways, through body language, speaking and writing. One of the most powerful parts of communication is the written word. Some words had little impact but others reach out to all aspects of human existence. The four letter word has such an impact. Examples include: Love, Hope, Life and Kiss to cite a few.

One word that caught my attention is the word *kiss*. This word permeates life, art, human relationships, love and even betrayal. Song writers like Victor Herbert wrote beautiful songs about a kiss including *Kiss Me Again, A Kiss in the Dark*, while Rudolph Friml wrote *One Kiss.* Poets too have written of the Kiss such as *Jenny Kissed Me* by Leigh Hunt. In the musical world there are so many operas and stage performance involving the kiss.

The flip side of this is the tragic use of the kiss in betrayal. The most egregious example is found in the Scriptures where Judas betrays Jesus with a kiss (Mk 14:44). This must be the most notorious use of the kiss in all human history.

There are a variety of kisses and a variety of meanings to a kiss. For example: kissing your mother-in-law, your child, a casual friend, or a treasured Rent-a-Daughter.

But, speaking of the kiss, can you remember the first time you kissed your true love?

I remember going out with Carol when we lived in California. I lived in Campbell near the railroad tracks and she lived in Atherton about 20 miles away where notables like Shirley Temple and Joe Montana live. So I drove her home and we sat in the driveway talking then I took her to the door and kissed her! WOW!

All the way home all I could think about was kissing her and it is a wonder I did not have an accident as I drove down the El Camino Real to Campbell. I always wonder how many auto accidents occur while pondering a first kiss.

Carol used to teach music and spent a lot of time in her studio. So in between students, I would sneak in and kiss her, just for the Love we shared.

Now at the first anniversary of her passing, I was thinking of the number of times I should have kissed her for all the Love she represented and the Love she shared with me, our children and her beloved students.

As Victor Herbert wrote and Beverly Sills sang, *"KISS ME AGAIN"*

NO CULTURE

When I was growing up in Hawaii during the Great Depression just getting through the day was a real accomplishment. We were fortunate that our church took care of our elementary education and my oldest brother, Wally, made it through the eighth grade, while my brother Paul the ninth grade. I flunked out in my first year of high school. Unfortunately, I spent more time playing and not studying.

Our cultural exposure was limited to attending Cowboy movies, listening to Hawaiian songs and Cowboy songs. Classical music was nowhere on our radar screen. We probably knew most of the Cowboy songs by heart and used to sing them. I have CD's of the Sons of the Pioneers that I often play.

My lack of culture went with me to California when one day, at San Jose State College, my friend Al Evans took me to the listening room and had me listen to Swan Lake. I was very pleased to hear that beautiful work, but never pursued music any further.

One of the significant events in life is the introduction of someone into your own life that can be a game changer. This happened to Johnny Cash who spent time in jail, but was a very talented musician and author. His "Folsom Prison Blues" preceded all of his concerts. He always wore black clothing, but eventually met June Carter who helped him turn his life around and made him a respected Christian and revered Western Music star as well as performer of Spiritual Music.

When I first met Carol I was overtaken by her and very much impressed with her love of music, arts and culture. She had begun teaching piano at age 15 and became a great teacher. She used to skip school and go to San Francisco to hear Artur Rubinstein concerts. In fact, she drew a portrait of him and presented it to him after a performance which he autographed and in turn gave her a picture of himself that she still has today.

One day she gave me a book "The Magic Bow" by Manuel Komroff. It was a story about Niccolo Paganini and a marvelous book. That was my introduction to the portals of some culture and I began to read poetry, listen to classical music and pay attention to the arts along with chemistry.

I am certain the reader has encountered people who have been path turner in their life and thank God for sending them across our life paths.

Thank you, Carol.

CHRISTOPHER J. BALLEW

Years ago Carol and I needed to have our towering oak trees trimmed. After searching for someone who could do that a friend suggested that we call Greg Ballew.

Greg showed up one morning to look over the project with his brother Chris who arrived in his jeep to assay the work. The operation required Chris to climb these towering oaks, trim the branches then Greg would show up after Chris left to pick up the branches and clean up after Chris.

Carol and I were amazed at the team work between these gentlemen. I would get nervous when I would see Chris high up an oak tree on the edge of a branch sawing away at branches that needed to be trimmed. Chris knew just what to trim and how to trim..a true expert.

One day I came home and found Chris at the top of a large white oak. When he saw me he came flying down to the ground on his rope. I was just amazed at his skill in climbing and descending these beautiful trees.

I used to teach at IUSB and one afternoon after class I came home and saw Chris standing in the yard with his eyes fixed to the woods and I wondered if there was a problem. I asked him what was up.

Chris replied, "Do you see them?"

I answered, "See what?"

Chris replied, "The trees".

Chris appeared mesmerized at the beauty of the trees and one would think that he was in a museum the way he was admiring the beauty of the trees.

This got me thinking of how we take for granted the marvelous gifts that God gives us. I shall never understand the beauty of the tree in its simplicity yet complex nature. Trees are made from sunlight, water and carbon dioxide. Yet they know how to repair themselves, when to drop leaves and to provide natural beauty and shelter.

Now I understand why Greg is so averse to cutting down trees and it pains me to see beautiful trees removed just for the sake of progress (?).

So thank you Chris for teaching me a real life Lesson in the beauty of God's Kingdom especially those giant oaks that reach up to Heaven.

God Bless You Chris and Rest in Peace.

LOVE OR HATE

The last of the Old Testament prophets, Malachi foretold the coming of Elijah and the terrible day of the Lord. Nothing much happened for 500 years, while the Israelites kept a sharp alert for the coming of the Messiah. Before Moses died he told his people that God would raise a prophet like him. So the Jews were watching for Elijah and the prophet. This is why when the Pharisees came to John the Baptist they asked him if he was Elijah or the Prophet. Jesus later confirmed that the Elijah that Malachi referred to was John the Baptist.

Jesus very important mission was to deliver the Kingdom of God to the people of the earth. John the Baptist declared that the Kingdom of God was at hand and shortly after that, when Jesus was baptized in the Jordan by John fulfilling that prophesy.

The Israelites were burdened by many laws and rules, similar to the United States now with too many costly regulations and little common sense. Jesus boiled all these laws down to a four word law: "**Love God, Love Neighbor**"

In four words, Jesus summed up the key to building a Kingdom of God as God had envisioned it, before the fall. What is frustrating is that the law is so simple, yet almost impossible to carry out in the current world situation.

Of more concern is that when Jesus left the Earth, He left a personal Faith that could be spread in a natural way by small growth, division and more growth. This is how bacteria grow by the process of cell division. The early Christians grew this way; as their numbers swelled, they split off to start new groups; spreading the faith through witnesses.

The Christian faith is based on Love; so much Love that Jesus gave His life to assure our eternal salvation! But, Jesus also warned us, before He left, that the 'Prince of this World' was coming and that Jesus had nothing to do with him

(Jn 14:30). So, the early church prospered based upon Love for about two hundred years until Satan moved in with his Kingdom whose foundation was based upon Hate!

For two thousand years now we have experienced the curse of Satan's Kingdom; wars; pestilence, poverty, hatred, greed, corruption and a world destined for destruction. When we search history and wonder how so many tyrants like Lenin, Hitler, Mao, Obama and others succeed, we wonder where they obtained so much power, that the ordinary leader would be banished in normal circumstances. The shadow government that is now trying to gain control of the world must derive their power from hate and not love.

At the current rate of degeneracy we must be living in an era of the End Times and the sooner we can replace the Kingdom of Hate with the Kingdom of Love, the better off the whole world will be.

As John said, "I come quickly" (Rev. 22:30)

Let us pray that it is sooner than later.

IS IT SATANIC?

*I*n a recent essay I discussed Possession regarding the success of famous people who seem to be above the moral base and the moral law. I cited notables like the current president, Bill and Hillary Clinton and leaders like Mao and Stalin who killed millions and walked free until Satan came to collect his consulting fee and they were destroyed. In another tale I mentioned the possibility of invoking satanic forces (demons) to do the work of people who practiced Black Religions like the Polynesians, Mayans, Egyptians and Aztecs. The remarkable stone structures they created seem to be beyond the capability of ordinary people.

During Jesus short life on earth, His first major encounter after baptism in the Jordan by John the Baptist, was with Satan who gave Jesus three irresistible offers. Fortunately for us, Jesus was able to overcome this demonic attack and continued His course to give us Eternal Salvation.

In every gospel account of Jesus mission He encounters demons that possess people and control their lives. One of the most significant encounters was when Jesus went to the land of the Gadarenes (Mk 5:1). Jesus encounters a man possessed who was terrorizing the area. When Jesus asked his name, the possessed man replied 'Legions" indicating that he was full of demons, not just one. Jesus expelled them into a herd of swine that ran into the sea and drowned.

Down through the ages we have record of demonic activities. Remember when Moses threw down his rod that turned into a serpent, the Egyptian magicians did the same. In Bram Stokers book, Dracula, he describes a fierce storm that erupted near the coast of England but the Russian schooner survived and found its way into port, so that Dracula could escape the ship as a dog.

So demons have the power to not only control animals or humans by possession, but can also affect natural phenomenon. (Remember that using spiritual power Jesus calmed the storm)!

Ever since the current president hit the public scene, his meteoric success seems to me to be powered by satanic forces. Consider his rise to power from obscurity to world wide acclaim. His lies match that of the Prince of Liars, Satan, and his escape from accountability is beyond reason.

While thinking about his satanic power I wondered if he (and his demons) brought on Sandy, the storm that detracted attention from the Libyan fiasco to cover him before the election.

You be the judge!

IS THIS OUR TIME?

After the Resurrection of our Lord Jesus Christ, the apostles still had difficulty in understanding the true mission of Jesus. They still believed that Jesus had come to restore the Kingdom to Israel. This was manifest when Jesus made His triumphal entry into Jerusalem. He was hailed as a political leader and not a spiritual leader. This was a big disappointment to Jesus who at that point realized that in spite of his three and a half year mission, the Israelites did not understand that He had preached a spiritual kingdom. After His forty days on earth, Jesus ascended into heaven and promised to return.

During the beginning of the early church, the apostles tried a communist system and this failed as the slackers began to take advantage of the ability to feed off the charity of true believers.(Acts 4:31-37).

As the apostles preached the Kingdom with great signs (Acts 3: 1-16) and wonders, the people began to expect the soon return of Christ. Later on, Paul preached to the Thessalonians that the Lord will come suddenly. (1Thess.4: 16-18). Paul then goes on to point out that the Lord will come without warning and when people least expects Him, He will return and they cannot escape His retribution. (1 Thess. 5: 1-10).

Since Paul's time, generations look at the state of affairs in their time and consider that the time of the end is near. This has lead to a gold mine for charlatans to preach the end times to fatten their treasures by fooling the gullible into giving up their money and fatten the wallets of these false prophets. These false prophets have made many predictions, even giving dates for the second coming only to be made foolish. Herbert W. Armstrong was one who made a prediction that Jesus would return and presented a specific date. Many of his supporters poured in their support (money) to this phony. When the appointed date came and went, he revised his date only to be proved wrong again.

"Beware of False Prophets "sums it up! (Matt. 7:15)

If we look at our current situation, we have the most corrupt government, immorality, and hardness of heart that the world has ever seen. Can this be the time of His return?

An encouraging sign is that all the prophesies have been fulfilled except the last one spoken by the angels at the ascension who promised His return in the same way that He ascended into heaven (Acts. 1:10,11).

How fortunate that we are living on the other side of the promise and do not have to wait for His first coming! We live in exciting times!

Come Lord Jesus Christ!

TREES

One of God's great gifts to us is the tree. The tree is a marvel of God's creativity and genius! Trees are the harbinger of Spring and a clue to the coming winter, when the level of sunlight is lower and the trees cease their production of chemicals like sugars, that make the tree by converting carbon dioxide and water into cellulose and lignin.

More remarkable is that the beautiful colors that make up the fall display are always present in the tree, but are masked by chlorophyll a bright green chemical. When photosynthesis ceases and no more chlorophyll is produced, we then see the other colors of fall.

If one were to examine the skeletal structure of a leaf, we would be overwhelmed by the complexity of the leaf with all of its branches of semi-permeable membranes that allow for the photosynthesis process. Yet, we are not always too kind toward leaves especially in the fall when we are overwhelmed by falling leaves and the chore of raking and disposing of them.

Have you ever considered the process by which a tree flourishes?

The tree operates by osmotic pressure, whereby the sugar laden roots attract water and push water and other chemicals up the tree to the leaves. Also amazing is how the tree can know the seasons, repair damage and provide shade, protection for wildlife and food for creatures of the forest.

Joyce Kilmer was so impressed with the tree that he wrote a memorable poem in which he declares that; "*I think that I shall never see, a poem lovely as a tree*". His poem was later put to song.

The tree is so important to mankind and participated in the most heinous act in civilization the instrument of execution of our Lord and Savior Jesus Christ. Legend has it that Christ was crucified on a dogwood tree. Eugene Field wrote a touching tale about the majestic dogwood that was chopped down to serve as Christ's cross. The tale goes on to say that after the death of Christ the dogwood became the minor tree that it is today.

The next time you can examine a dogwood, you will see a crown on the center of the flower, leaves that develop a red edge indicating Christ's blood and a final red before shedding its leaves.

Trees then are a remarkable example of God's kingdom, marvelous in their chemistry and a constant reminder of the majesty of our God.

DANIEL

After the Israelites escaped from Egypt, they finally reached the Promised Land, led by Joshua, who had taken over leadership when Moses died. The Israelites are a very stiff necked people who gave Moses a hard time all the way from Egypt to the Jordan. Eventually, God sent Judges, Sampson, and then Prophets to remind the Israelites of the promises of God and how to keep themselves in God's favor. The Israelites had a standard treatment for God's Prophets. They stoned them or hung them on a tree. (One would wonder, if it is safe for Jesus to again return, based upon past history?)

One of the great prophets was Daniel. He was captured by King Nebuchadnezzar when the Babylonians overwhelmed Israel and took a remnant to Babylon. Daniel and his companions confounded the Babylonians by showing them that their dietary laws produced better results than those of those pagans (Dan.1:11-21). Daniel proved to be right and gained the favor of King Nebuchadnezzar and made him a ruler over the entire province of Babylon!

Later on, the King had an awesome dream that has ramifications to this very day. The King had a terrible dream, such that he was visibly shaken and very scared. But, he could not remember the dream and his soothsayers could not reproduce the dream, or its interpretation. Eventually, Daniel came forth and disclosed the dream, then gave the interpretation thereof. The King was overwhelmed and made Daniel a recognized prophet. (Dan. 2) This prophecy is very significant because Daniel described the current situation in our crumbling world. The king had dreamed of a fierce statue with a head of gold, a chest of silver, belly bronze, legs of iron and feet composed of iron and clay. Daniel further prophesied that a stone would strike the feet of the statue and destroy it. The head of gold represented King Nebuchadnezzar, while the lesser metals represented other kingdoms in descending order of importance. Some think that the feet of clay and iron represent the European Union and the rock that destroys them, the power of God at Christ's return.

Daniel, like most prophets, had a lot of enemies. Some of the Babylonians drew up a law to force Daniel and his friends to worship a statue. Daniel and his companions refused and the King was forced to condemn them to be punished. And so Shadrach, Meshach and Abednego (not to be confused with A Bad Negro) were cast into a fiery furnace, but were saved (Dan Ch3). The King was stunned to see the three walking around unharmed but a fourth person was seen; likened to the Son of Man.

Engineers have studied the type of furnace used to burn the Israelites and have found that there is a cool zone in the furnace and that explains why they were saved. However, I prefer to believe in the power of the Almighty who provided for their safety.

Daniel's last prophecy involved a prediction of the last days in which there will be a period of travail lasting some 1,290 days or for times, times and half a time or three and a half years.

Surely, Daniel accurately predicted our day when he, in Chapter 12 predicted:

"From the time that the daily sacrifice is abolished and the Obamination that causes desolation is set up, there will be 1,290 days"

Are we there yet?

THROWN OUT OF THE TENT

Patrick Buchanan recently published a book, "Suicide of a Super Power" in which he lists some disturbing consequences of our stupidity in turning our great nation from a great Federal Republic to a waning Third Rate Country. He cites cases going back to the Founding Fathers who warned us of the dangers of not being vigilant, reckless spending, an ever expanding government meddling in foreign nation's affairs, undeclared wars, illegal immigration and bad trade policies. Sadly, we are witnessing the fulfillment of these early warnings and appear totally incapable of turning the country around.

Every night our TV sets offer us a parade of experts who try to analyze what is going on and to offer solutions. In most cases, these experts have their own axe to grind and are part of the problem. The media bias allows only talking points agenda items to be discussed and the truth is ridiculed and many who speak the truth, like Buchanan and Juan Williams have paid a dear price by crossing the line in speaking the truth. In both cases these men lost their jobs and are pilloried by the Left Wing Media.

In a similar manner we watch our moral ship slowly and now rapidly disappearing beneath the waters of our moral sewer as we sit silently by and permit loud voices to convince us that we must be tolerant of abhorrent behavior and practices. The foul language now used in radio and television would have resulted in public outrage back two generations ago. I can recall when there was a huge fuss over the word 'damn' used by Clark Gable in Gone with the Wind. Today, perverse behavior and language is tolerated as normal.

How did we get to this stage of decay?

In our history books we often read of the fall of great empires and the base causes that lead to the failure. In the Roman case, it began with illegal immigration when the Romans offered sanctuary to people fleeing the barbarians. The saved people, instead of adopting Roman culture, as required kept their culture and the race over the cliff to the ash heap of history began. This was followed with debasement of the currency and wine and then on to moral decay as described in the first chapter of Romans by St. Paul. The cheaper wines were more acidic and extracted lead from their pewter drinking vessels causing brain damage. (Remember Nero fiddling while Rome burned?)

We too can look to a simple cause of our moral, spiritual and national failure in one simple act where the Supreme Court threw God out of our schools with the Brown v Board of Education! Since then we have begun our race to the end. This has a precedent in the Old Testament. The Israelites had God for their King. Whenever they set up the tent containing the Ark of the Covenant, God's presence could be seen as a cloud that hovered above the tent. Then they asked for a visible King and God gave them Saul. As a result they threw God out of the tent and it has been a disaster ever since.

When and until we restore God in our everyday life we must live with the same sense of security enjoyed by the passengers on the *Titanic*.

CROSSING THE BULL PEN

When I lived in Honolulu we rarely wore shoes. I have a picture of my fourth grade class at Cathedral School where we were all required to wear ties to school, but went barefoot. Because of this practice we tended to develop thick skin on the bottom of our feet, but not thick enough to prevent stick weeds or thorns to give us a real pain.

My Uncle Joe (Double Rope) had a dairy near Kaneohe that he leased from Harold Castle. Double Rope had about 130 milking cows ranging from Holsteins, Guernsey, Jersey and Ayrshires . The Holsteins were large cows usually black and white and produced the most milk. The Guernsey and Jersey cows had the most butter fat in their milk.

Uncle Joe's dairy was at the bottom of a valley and ended in a swamp next to a banana patch. The dairy was laid out with living quarters for the milkmen, a large bull pen and sectioned off areas where the cows were pastured. Beyond the fenced area were many guava bushes and the cows would wander into the bushes.

The cows knew what time milking would begin and would line up by the gate of the foot washer. Some cows did not always show up so my brother Paul and I had to round up the stray cows. This required us to search the bushes for any that did not show up on time.

Enter *Mimosa pigra,*

This invasive weed has sharp thorns and when touched will fold up its leaves leaving the thorns more exposed and dangerous for bare footed cow chasers. The Bull Pen was covered with these weeds and when we walked through the bull pen we felt like a swami lying on a bed of spikes. So we found a way to ease our pain by seeking out dried cow pies. After sitting in the sun the cow pies hardened so we could stand on them and avoid the weed thorns.

Unfortunately, we were not always that lucky since some of the cow pies appeared to be dry but we soon found our feet sinking down and the processed cow feed came gushing up through our toes. Not a pleasant experience.

In our own lives we sometimes make the same mistakes as walking across the bull pen by uttering the wrong word or sentence that can be very embarrassing. Two examples will suffice:

My friend Tom took his girl friend Andrea home and kissed her goodnight saying, "Good night Phyllis"

I have two Greyhounds and they leave a lot of fossils around their pen and I have to scoop them up. My dear friend Donna has four dogs and I try to imagine her situation when she has to clean her yard. So one day I casually mentioned to her that whenever I pick up fossils I think of her. **HOW ROMANTIC**!

So be careful when you cross the bull pen; you never know that when trying to avoid a Mimosa weed you might just step on a soft cow pie.

EASIER SAID THAN DONE

When friends ask me for help, I usually remind them to Trust in God and He will see you through your trouble. Over the years, Carol and I have found this to be our rock in difficult times and we have enough examples of the times God has responded to our prayers.

Yet, one of the biggest problems is that it is easy to say, but many times our faith is not strong enough to overcome the tendency to deny the very faith I like to talk about. For me this week was a real test, and I am afraid that my faith was severely tested and I came very close to giving up.

On Thursday night our Greyhound, Miki, bolted and ran away into the woods. I quickly drove to a place where I knew she would go in Woodland Hills, but she was not there. As it was getting dark, I had to give up the search. There was a thunderstorm brewing and poor Miki was gone.

After searching on Friday, there was no clue that I would ever see her again. I called Irene and Donna for help and they responded, as usual, with great care and love to help me find Miki. I then went to see Carol to ask her for assistance, because since she died, Carol has always answered my prayers. I spent all of Friday visiting the Animal Shelters and spreading the word about Miki.

On Saturday, I did my visits to the Animal shelters and Donna and Spenser were preparing posters with Miki's picture and information. About two in the afternoon I called Irene and told her I was giving up on ever seeing her again, and Irene chided me for my lack of faith. As I was chatting with her my home phone rang and it was a caller who had found Miki at the Granger Community Church soccer field and took her home. It did not take long to retrieve my wayward Greyhound.

In retrospect, I am ashamed of myself for being so quick to lose faith as I should have known that God always answers prayer. So I went to see Carol at the cemetery to tell her the good news and when I returned there was a large truck in the driveway. It was Dale and Donna who had brought over a fence to prevent this from happening again.

This is certainly a lesson in humility to witness the Love and Care real friends have for me and others. When God sent Dale and Donna into our lives, we never anticipated what real love can be for people who care. Irene's Love and Care also make life so much richer.

Trust in the Lord Always and don't give up so soon, Tom!

END OF THE WORLD

A very interesting phenomenon is the curiosity of people to consider the possibility of the World coming to an end. Some of this anxiety is biblically based see (II Pet. 3:10; I Thess 4:16 and 5: 1-3) and have been used by charlatan preachers and hucksters to scare Christians into giving up their worldly possessions (to the church of course) and await the end. Preachers like Herbert W. Armstrong had predicted the end of the world twice after his first date did not show.

When I was growing up my Mother told us a story of some charlatan in Hilo spreading the word that the end was near and many of the stupid folks sold all their belongings and waited for the end. Jesus warned us to be ever vigilant but would not ever predict the timing, since He said that only the Father knows.

As the year 2000 approached many were predicting dire consequences for our power grid, the computer system and many other facets of our society. In fact Governor Huckabee had developed a task force of his key staff to await the big calamity that was supposed to occur as the last century came to a close. After midnight, they discovered that nothing happened and he dismissed his staff and went home.

I once wrote an essay for our Bible Group at Whirlpool, "The Second Coming" the topic of world ending suggesting that we should be ever vigilant; actually what Jesus and the prophets had spoken in the past.

Presently, we are facing the worst situation the world has ever seen; like the fulfillment of the prophesy of St. Paul in II Tim 3: 1-7) where the apostle promised perilous time are coming. I may now get back to my early essay predicting the end of the world and this time I and my good friend Steve Kash are on the right track. Regardless of prophesy and scripture I feel that I can predict the end of the world this time and give you the date:

NOVEMBER 6, 2012.

Preventing a calamity like this is almost impossible. Remember when Jonah the Prophet told the people of Nineveh that "yet forty days and Nineveh will be destroyed". The king repented in ashes and sack cloth and Nineveh was spared.

Can we in the United States prevent the end of the world as we know it? Many organizations are trying to prevent this from happening but many, like the Catholic Church, are using limp wristed methods to stop this tragedy, instead of calling out the monster responsible for our peril.

There is one chance to stop this calamity of November 6 and that is voters must rise and send this president back to the dark pit from which he arose and those like him.

So it is up to you to save the world: Pray and VOTE!

NEAR THE END

*A*nother major earthquake today near the coast of Japan! This one was 7.1 on the Richter scale and occurred on the ocean floor. The world has been shaken with enormous quakes over the last several years. These calamities of the earth's crust are accompanied by civil unrest, perpetual wars, famine, disease (the Ebola virus has now spread to all continents) and is uncontrollable. Several new diseases have migrated into the United States from Mexico and causing a major health crisis in California and Arizona. To add to this volcanoes around the world are erupting at an enormous rate. Volcanologists are concerned about the Three Sister Volcanoes near Bend Oregon. More alarming is the increasing temperature of Mt. Rainier which could melt the glaciers and flood the valleys below. Geologists fear that the Pacific Coast Volcanoes might erupt like the ancient Mt. Mazama that created Crater Lake in Oregon.

To add to this picture we are witnessing a global shortage of water and the UN is acting to take over the Great Lakes to supply to Third World Countries in an effort to stem the global famine where millions are dying. The United States is in turmoil because of riots in its major cities and politicians are unable to stop them. Most of the politician's efforts have been devoted to stamping out Christianity in our schools and daily lives leaving little resources to combat civil disruptions. Some Christians who are bold enough to see the hand of God in these dangerous times have been arrested for creating fear among the populace.

Meanwhile, with the eruption of so many volcanoes, the sun is rarely seen as the air becomes more laden with sulfurous gases. The UN has voted a punishing tax on all nations to stop the pollution with the Western Countries required to carry the bulk of the burden.

Meanwhile, the churches stricken with a large deficit of funds because the people are so heavily taxed have devoted many sermons to the need to prop up the coffers of the churches, lest they go bankrupt. The faithful however move closer to their bibles to study Matt. 24 and II Tim. 3:1-7 to realize what is going on.

With all the grief and sorrow in the world, one day the world is shocked by an interruption of TV stations around the world with this headline:
JESUS CHRIST AND A HOST OF ANGELS HAVE JUST ARRIVED IN JERUSALEM TWENTY MINUTES AGO! NOW BACK TO OUR COVERAGE OF SANDRA FLUKE AND HER AGENDA TO OBTAIN FREE CONTRACEPTIVES FOR WOMEN.

Things began to happen fast. The General Secretary of the UN rushed to Jerusalem to advise Jesus that He is not welcome here as his values are completely out of line with those of this world. The SG is banished with one word from our Savior, "Begone" and that was the end of the UN, Meanwhile the UN building collapses into the East River and the devils headquarters are banned forever.

For the rest of the story read Revelations.

HE HAS NO ARMY

*J*esus promised the apostles that there would be wars and rumors in his discourse concerning the end times (Matt. 24: 6,7). If we study the history of the world, we learn that wars are a natural consequence of man's rebellion against God beginning with the loss of our salvation in the Garden of Eden.

In our recent past we have seen a continuous wave of wars beginning with World War I. This was a 'war to end all wars', but that did not last long. The planners and schemers who direct world conflict began planning their next war soon after 1918, even selecting the warring partners giving us World War II. By this time, the true hand of Satan was shown as we launched into a series of endless and winless wars.

Nations began to spend their treasure on developing the most sophisticated weapons of mass destruction and the perpetual wars were a great testing ground to prove the effectiveness of these weapons!

Nations rely on building large amounts of weaponry to either pursue aggressive action on other nations or to put fear into adversaries to prevent war. President Reagan built our military in the face of the Soviet threat and was successful in stopping the Soviet Nuclear threat to the United States.

In ancient times superior nations would build up large armies and march against their adversaries who in many cases were overwhelmed or lacked the army to fight the oppressors.

During the reign of King Hezekiah, the Assyrians planned to attack Israel. God promised that he would defend the city (Isa. 37:35). One would ask, "With no army, how could God protect the city?"

When Sennacherib descended upon the city with 185.000 troops, it looked bad for the people of the city. Yet, Sennacherib's whole army was destroyed in the night and the city was saved (Isa.37:36).

The description by Isaiah is that an angel of the Lord swept through the camp and destroyed the Assyrians. A likely explanation is that the Assyrian Army was overcome by smallpox.

What Christians must do is pay strict attention to the treasure in the Bible and watch for signs in the heavens that might indicate His near coming. God through His prophets has indicated the signs of the end times and we are told to watch.

In all our pride and technology, we tend to become arrogant and are working to achieve what only God can do. Witness the sale of body parts of aborted babies and our dropping morality. We are saying to God that with our now superior understanding, we can break God's laws with impunity.

Remember all the military strength in the world is no match for God!

Unless we turn to God for forgiveness, we are doomed and God has no army, but He will win.

DOES PRAYER WORK?

One of my thoughts on prayer is that prayer works, but in God's good time. Another truth is that the most important time to pray is when things are going well, because when things turn bad, we can use the accumulated grace of previous prayer to obtain an answer to prayer. Finally, God does answer all prayer; but He also says No and we must accept that.

To illustrate, years ago I was in a bad job situation and had no good alternative to escape my consequences. I also faced imminent drafting into the Army and stopped by at church each night to pray to God to save me from the Draft. Here God said No, and for good reason. Had He said yes, I would have never received the education I needed to succeed in the Scientific World.

We are also taught to pray always (Lk 18:1). And, when we pray we must have a totally committed Faith that our prayer will be answered. St. James chastises us about praying with Faith (Jas. 1:6) and to keep our Faith unwavering!

Last Sunday I was given the opportunity to test the power of prayer, the Love of Friends, and Faith in the promised word of Jesus and His Saints. I lost Miki our Greyhound and being a stormy night, the odds of finding her were dismal.

It was then I remembered the Faith that Carol had in Jesus and her devotion to Sr. Faustina who gave us the Chaplet that is devoted to prayer and was dictated to her by Jesus Himself. So I prayed the Chaplet for her safe return and laid down a challenge to my Faith that I would believe that Miki would be returned.

Meanwhile, I asked our good friends Sharon and Carl Borek for prayer and they responded by combing a large area to search for her. (Christian Love at its best!).

The next morning I had a rather calm feeling to my loss and while calling Dog Shelters, the phone rang and I was told that Miki had been found:

Praise the Lord! She had been hit by a car on Grape Road and suffer some minor injuries, but will survive.

The only conclusion one can derive from this experience that Faith, Love and Prayer does work and when we walk in His presence we can reap the rewards that prayer, Faith and Love give to those who trust in Him.

"God gives His Best to those who leave the choice with Him"

WORSE THAN EDEN

One of the most beautiful stories in the Bible is the description of the creation! Here in a few chapters, Moses describes the creation of the universe and ends with the complete Garden of Eden. Moses describes this major feat as a period of six days, when God created Adam and Eve in His image and likeness. In God's perfect Kingdom, He set mankind for an eternity of living in Paradise. With this gift, and any gift from God, there are caveats. What God demanded was that Adam and Eve live in a manner that he proscribed and set rules of behavior. One of God's strictest rules is that we must never disobey God!

Enter Satan!

Things were going well until Satan entered the picture. We must remember that Satan is extremely powerful, both materially and spiritually, and that in our time is in control of our world. (If you wonder what kind of a leader Satan would be, we just need to reflect on our own situation with the leadership we now have!)

The Kingdom of God in Eden was based upon Love, good behavior and respect for God's laws. Satan could not abide this type of competition and set out to destroy it. His temptation was so great that no one could overcome it, except Jesus, as He did in the desert. We are all familiar with the result and we have lived with the consequence of that sin since the expulsion from Paradise. Fortunately, we are promised a redeemer and He indeed came and died for us on the cross.

Meanwhile, back with the Israelites, we see a number of human follies as the Israelites are a stiff necked people and often disobedient to God. Some of their follies include selling themselves to slavery by giving up their freedom for pottage, sort of like Esau. So God had to free the Israelites and sent Moses to lead them to the Promised Land. But the Israelites rebelled again and had to spend forty years in the desert until the old folks died. After that God finally gave the Israelites a kingdom, but not for long.

The Israelites prospered as long as God was their King. But in 1Samuel 8, we find the Israelites falling back on their own wicked ways. Instead of being content with God as their King, they wanted to be like other nations. As a result they rejected God and asked for a King that they could see, just as the other fallen nations. God was displeased, but gave them a king, Saul and they returned to bondage. (1Sam.8:6-18). As a result we have been slaves to Satan ever since.

This decision by the Israelites displeased the prophet Samuel and denied us of an opportunity of having a government ruled by God Himself and worse than the tragedy of Eden.

Now we must wait for the Second Coming to finally straighten us out.

BE CAREFUL WHAT YOU ASK FOR…YOU MAY GET IT

CONTRACEPTION

One of the tenets of the Catholic Church is the battle against contraception. The Church uses the 'Sin of Onan' (Gen 38:8-10) as an example of God's wrath on Onan who failed to complete a required sex act with his brother's widow as required by law. In addition, the Church insists on the only method of birth control is the natural method which is about 99% successful.

The strict application of the Church's teachings in this area is a matter of serious concern. One good aspect of restricting artificial methods of conception control is that this produces a large number of children in a Catholic family and that in turn permits Catholics to dominate in a given culture. (The Muslims practice this approach and will dominate where ever their numbers increase). Good examples of this are in France and England where whole cities that were French or English look more like Middle Eastern cities then the native population. In third world countries there is a preponderance of children and in most cases they are starving and diseased. Efforts to teach contraception are strongly opposed by churches, while the hunger and misery goes on.

A thinking person would look at this situation and wonder why the Creator gave us the knowledge to control the population such that resources can meet the demands of the population.

A noted Technological Forecaster, Richard C. Davis, once gave a speech entitled "*Let them Starve*" to the consternation of many in his audience. He presented a scenario where there was a twenty nine year old man starving in the gutters of Calcutta. Good intentioned people would rush to feed him and he would reward the do-gooders by producing five more starving people.

In this writer's view, there is a major disconnect between the definition of birth control and conception control. Birth control (abortion) is the ending of a viable life and is nothing more than 'murder spelled sideways' and should not be tolerated in any society. On the other hand, conception control does not destroy a living entity. The sperm as well as the ovum have a limited life but cannot exist like a fertilized egg.

Why would God give us the intellect to understand the reproductive process and a way to circumvent the tragedy of overpopulation? The use of conception control needs to be balanced by strong moral restraints to prevent abuse for personal gratification.

Pity the poor family who are saddled with another 'gift from God' when they cannot provide for the existing family and the Church's attitude that "God will provide". Their goal is to satisfy an agenda with little or no concern for the unfortunate children.

"There is nothing more frightening than ignorance in action"
Goethe

LOOKING FOR A KING

Years ago Telly Savalas, a noted Hollywood actor, was on his way to Greece to be honored there for his contributions to the film industry. As he boarded his plane and sat in the First Class section, an elderly gentleman came to him and told Telly that he admired his acting talent. Telly was not impressed and wondered when this old man would leave him alone. During the long flight to Athens, the elderly gentleman came to Telly a number of times to rave about his acting skills much to the annoyance of Mr. Savalas.

When they finally arrived, Mr. Savalas was eager to depart to the accolades of his fans. But the stewardess asked him to remain seated as there was a notable figure aboard and that individual is exiting first. The old man arose from his seat and walked out of the plane to the sound of a band and cheers from the crowd.

You see the old man was the King of Greece!

In the Bible Peter reminds us that "we should humble ourselves under the mighty Hand of God" (I Pet 5,6).and I am certain that this good advice would have served Mr. Savalas well.

Each spring we relive the Lenten Season reminding us of the passion and death of Jesus Christ. We also witness sadly the inability of the people who could not recognize who Jesus really was. More sadly those in the know, the Pharisees, had the knowledge of the prophets and indeed knew who Jesus was; the Son of God. The problem facing the rulers of the Jews was that Jesus was a threat to their power over the people and their source of income!

Jesus came to bring the Kingdom of God and to fulfill the prophecies related to Him to the lost people in Israel. In this He was the fulfillment of the promise of Moses before he died. God tried to remind the Israelites of His promise to Abram and to the covenant by sending first Judges, then prophets. Unfortunately, the prophets told the truth and this was very detrimental to the health of prophet, since the people killed them.

Later Jesus spoke of a King sending his servants to obtain the fruits of his vineyard only to have them abused and finally killed. In this last tale, Jesus was referring to Himself and the rulers of the people knew that Jesus was talking about them (Lk. 20: 9-19).

We have had so many warnings; will we heed the message of the Scriptures?

GO TO THE TOP

People face many problems in life and one of these is dealing with a product that is not functioning as it should. At the present time we are looking at many automobile recalls for faulty parts or components. General Motors is facing an inquiry concerning their ignition switches that has brought about a congressional investigation. Congress went to the top and questioned the Chairman.

When products fail, the customers must follow a set procedure developed by the firm who provided the product and customers are usually referred to a Customer Service function to resolve whatever issue is extant. Having the product fixed is usually handled well by concerned organizations, while in other situations, customers can be frustrated by delays or what seems to be either an indifference or incompetent response by those assigned to fix the problem. The usual pathway to solution involves going over the head of the one assigned to the problem and hopefully up the chain to achieve satisfaction.

I recall purchasing a washing machine that had many defects and I was unable to achieve satisfaction from the dealer. Finally, I phoned the Chairman of the Company and spoke to him directly and obtained satisfaction. I did remember to call him back to thank him for his quick and effective intervention. Going to the top was very effective in this case.

This same situation can and does occur in the spiritual aspects of our lives. Many times in life we are faced with serious situations that appear to be beyond our ability to solve. Here we are advised to turn to prayer for assistance. Prayer is a most effective solution to many problems and prayer works! Jesus advised us to pray always.

In the Catholic Church we honor Mary and the Saints and are urged to turn to these as intercessors for our physical and spiritual needs. We are told that we need the intercession of saints to have access to God's divine mercy.

But, why do we need to go to these sources for help when Jesus is available to us always. It was Jesus who died upon the cross for our salvation and all things were made by Him and without Him nothing was made (Jn. 1:3). We are blessed to have this access to Jesus (like calling on the Chairman of the Board for quick action) who hears our prayers and answers them. A word of caution is that Jesus answers prayer in His due time and that may not satisfy our lust for instant gratification. But when Jesus answers He gives more than that for which we asked.

We must thank God for giving us the path to solution of our problems and that we can go directly to Him with our needs. And whatever you do, do not forget to thank Him. Remember the Samaritan leper who was cured and had the common sense to thank Jesus publicly, while the other nine were more interested in their own selves and could not take time to thank Jesus for curing their leprosy (Lk 17.12-19).

So when you have a need go directly to the top…and get amazing results.

CHRISTIAN LIBERTY AND THE UNBORN

In one of St. Paul's beautiful epistles he charges us to "Pray without ceasing" (1 Thess 5:17).
Throughout the scriptures we are urged to pray. The apostles who looked to Jesus for guidance came to Jesus and asked Him to teach them to pray. Little did the apostles realize what a response they would receive from our Lord of Lords.

Jesus gave them the Lord's Prayer the most beautiful spiritual and material prayer of all time. (Matt. 6: 9-14). This prayer overshadowed all the prayers and hype of the Pharisees who loved to stand on the street corners and pray to impress others and not the God of Heaven.

Today we need prayer more than ever as we watch our world crumble before us economically and morally. We have thrown out biblical principles for self satisfying needs disregarding the tenets of a good moral society. We have taken the gift of life and trivialized it to point whereby we give little or no thought to the sanctity of life. While we cite the terrible losses of life in the 20th century where millions were killed and then build museums to mourn the loss of lives building Holocaust Museums to remind us of the horror of war. Where are the museums for the unborn?

Today we have a more dangerous war facing us; a war between Satan and the innocent unborn! We have turned our backs on the innocent in the womb and offered them up for slaughter in the name of Roe v Wade, a Woman Right to Health Care and have relabeled murder by calling it choice.

This is a lie and one that the Father of Lies would support.

The ancients would sacrifice their babies to the god Marduk in a horrible manner. A fire was built under the outstretched hands of the god and a child placed in the hot hands; killing at least two each day. Reading about this horror is revolting, but we are doing the same only by the millions and counting.

We are here today to offer prayers to our Lord Jesus Christ to save us and our unborn. We need to pray not only for the innocents crying from the womb, but for ourselves for allowing this carnage to continue all around us.

How can we expect Jesus to hear our prayers, when our hands are dripping with the blood of the innocents?

Yes we thank God today for His mercy, but we must rise up and defend the innocents and storm the gates of government to end this carnage.

St. James speaks of Faith without works is of no value. We need to put our Faith and prayers to work to stop this savagery now. The Church must lead the way and the faithful with the help of Almighty God must stop this outrage, exert pressure on those who can stop the carnage.

Lord give us the resolve and courage to free the innocent from Death's grip, save our own souls and become children of God who will answer our prayers after we do what is right for the Unborn.

A TESTIMONY

"Let the words of my mouth and the meditation of my heart be acceptable in you sight, Oh, Lord my strength and my Redeemer"

There are many examples where Faith overcomes obstacles in our lives. Some events are not spectacular, while others may border on the miraculous side. I recently had the opportunity to share this story with a church group to illustrate what Faith can do for one who believes.

About fifteen years ago, my dear wife of 58 years was struck with a case of a rare form of follicular thyroid cancer. The doctors informed us that there were only two cases in our area and those patients died within two months. The tumor settled on her spine and she became an invalid. After a surgery in Indianapolis, they removed the tumor, but she was told that she would be confined to a wheel chair for the rest of her life. This was a crushing blow, since is an avid gardener and spent many hours among her flowers and plants.

Every evening after we finished our prayers, she would lie in bed and pray to Jesus that if she could only touch the hem of His garment, she would walk again.

At that time we were attending a Melkite Orthodox church and one Sunday we had a visiting priest who gave a sermon about healing. Fr. Taft told of a Belgian man who was injured in a logging accident and unable to walk. The priest asked the man what he was going to do about his situation. The man told the priest that he was saving money so he could go to Lourdes to be healed. The priest told him that Jesus is everywhere and that he need not go to Lourdes, since he could be healed in Belgium.

The man rose up and walked!

After the service, Carol handed me her walker and took my hand and walked out to the car. When we arrived home, we walked over to our neighbor's home and they were shocked to see Carol walking. She could walk from then on until her death ten years later.

To thank God for His mercy, Carol named her garden God's Garden. Karen Clifford wrote a story in Today's Catholic to commemorate Carol's Blessing.

If we consider the words in Psalm 19:14 cited above, we must realize that we must make a concerted effort each day to comply with the thought in this verse.

We walk a tightrope to salvation, and without the ever presence of Jesus Christ in our life, we can fall off that tight rope and be lost. Fortunately for us, Jesus is ever present and available to us always. We just need to keep our thoughts and spirit to be in tune with Him.

PURGATORY

The Catechism of the Catholic Church describes Purgatory as *'a state of final purification after death and before entrance into Heaven for those who died in God's friendship, but were only imperfectly purified; a final cleansing of human imperfection before one is able to enter into the joy of heaven'*. (Cat. 1031).

For an inquiring mind this leads to a number of questions concerning the concept of Purgatory, to wit:

- What is the biblical proof of the existence of purgatory?
- If Jesus died for our sins on the cross, why do we need to go to purgatory?
- The Church offers indulgences to bail out sinners in purgatory; so when do we know when the sinner has had enough indulgences to move on to heaven?
- The issue of indulgences caused the great Protestant Revolution.

From my limited knowledge of the bible, I have not found any references to Purgatory in any of the books of the bible. The closest I can find is the reference to the Rich Man and Lazarus in which Lazarus describes a large gulf between the living and the dead (Lk 16: 20-26). What Luke describes is in reality a description of hell and not Purgatory.

Jesus Christ was the sacrificial lamb who died for our sins as an ultimate and final sacrifice for all time. In His dying on the cross, Jesus opened the gates of heaven to sinners and put an end to animal sacrifice for all time. I cannot recall in any of the New Testament writings, Jesus referring to Purgatory.

The Catholic Church teaches that when a person dies, they go to Purgatory, prior to going to heaven. Where in the scriptures is that taught? The Church developed the concept of indulgences to work as bail bonds to help free souls from Purgatory; none of this teaching is in the bible. So how do we know how many indulgences are required to free a soul? Is there an indulgence amount to every sin like a bail bond? And of course, when and how do we know when a soul's ransom is paid. I always thought that Jesus paid our ransom on the cross.

One is only needed to be reminded of Martin Luther who questioned the issue of indulgences and paid a large price. Luther smelled a rat and challenged the Pope by nailing his '95 Theses' to the door of the Wittenberg Catholic Church that included his criticisms of selling indulgences by the Catholic Church thus setting off the Protestant Revolution.

There are so many controversies over Organized Religions that we do not need fables to justify our faith in the Lord Jesus Christ. Jesus is our salvation; it's straight forward and needs no tales to support his Love for us by dying for us on the Cross of Salvation.

HOW CAN THIS BE?

A remarkable aspect of the Holy Bible is that there are many events that defy logical explanations. For example, the birth of Jesus in Bethlehem predicted by Micah (Mich. 5:2), the parting of the Red Sea, the replenishment of oil and meal for Elias and Jesus walking on the sea or feeding five thousand with two loaves and a few fish. Critics try to find logical explanations to no avail until they accept the Divine Nature of Jesus.

Throughout the Scriptures we are given symbolisms, such as the Great Statue that King Nebuchadnezzar had seen in his dream (Dan 2) . But, the stature did have meaning and it took Daniel to explain the dream and its meaning. Other examples can be cited, but this should suffice to carry on with this tale.

If one was to look at the Bible Timeline, it is quite obvious that we are near the end of the world as we know it and as described in the Revelation of St. John written about 90 A.D. If we search the scriptures, we can see that most of the major prophecies have now been fulfilled. One of the prophecies from Mark indicates that the gospel must be preached to all nations, then the end will come (Mark.13:10). During the height of the Roman Empire, worldwide communications were at their best, and that allowed Christianity to be spread all over the known world. With satellite communication today, there is little reason not to believe that the gospel has been preached to all nations.

An amazing prediction of John (Rev. 16:12) predicts the drying of the Euphrates River. Should this happen the armies of China could move into the Levant and attack Israel. How could John have known this, two thousand years before it happened? (One of the signs of a true prophet is that they are never wrong). How could this mighty river go dry? One of the answers is the Anatolia Project in Turkey which will have the ability to choke off the waters of the Tigris and Euphrates Rivers, thus drying them up as John predicts.

People today are facing daily onslaughts of bad news and many are trying to understand what is going on. People who study the world scene and understand what is going on are labeled "Conspiracy Nuts". But, before we criticize these we should remember that things just don't happen by chance and are planned far into the future by those determined to rule the world.

To illustrate, during the Cold War American Foreign Aid was sent to Afghanistan where a concrete highway was built from Kabul to the Soviet Border. Why? Soon after, America sent an entire truck manufacturing plant to Russia. These trucks were needed for the projected invasion of Kabul many years later. Similarly, the invasion of poor children from Central America is being sold to us as poor children whose parents are paying $5,000 per child to migrate to America. Where are they getting this money and if they are poor wouldn't they be better off at home?

So much of what we are witnessing today is being directed by the Prince of Lies, Satan, whose time is running short. Christians must be prepared to recognize what is happening and gird themselves with the Gospel of Truth.

IDOLATRY

When God gave the law to Moses, God wrote His law on stone in the form of the Ten Commandments (Ex. 20). After announcing who He is, God proceeds to charge the Israelites to "have no strange gods before me" Ex 20: 3-5. Why would God put such a great emphasis on this?

In the pagan world, the Romans had gods like Diana, goddess of the moon, hunt, birthing and wild animals or Venus the goddess of love, beauty, sex, fertility, prosperity and desire. The Greek had their share of gods in Apollo, god of prophesy and healing and Testicles, god of sex.

After the fall, people soon turned to Idolatry worshiping animals, statues, false gods (Amalek) and soon descended into satanic worship. This is an easy task for humans as Satan is the driving force behind Idolatry and many fall for this nonsense as witnessed in the present day.

Now why would God put this so high on His list of commandments?

In order to understand this, we need to probe into the being of God. Isaiah provides an excellent discussion about the person of God (Isa 40). A serious reading of this remarkable chapter gives the reader a better comprehension of the person and spirituality of God. It is almost beyond understanding to attempt to understand how significant God is and how there is no other God like him. Consider the Creator of the Universe and all therein, the fact that God understands the total nature of all creatures, their structure, physiology, metabolism in its infinite detail is mind boggling.

To know in complete detail the complete organism would be a monumental task, yet consider that God fully understands all creatures, all minerals, plants and all that exists in the physical and spiritual world gives us some glimpse of why God is so opposed to idolatry.

What makes idolatry so dangerous is the ease in which we can fall into that trap. Worse yet, even after a major event where God has rescued the

Israelites from the grip of Pharaoh, saw them across the Red Sea and freed them from bondage, they soon resorted to Idolatry when Moses went up to Mt. Sinai to receive the Law, they built a Golden Calf and fell into Idolatry.

How could the Israelites be so stupid?

They were no better than we are today. We are so steeped into Idolatry, that it is a small wonder that the Wrath of God has not yet engulfed us. We worship people of low morality, actors, public figures and entertainers as though they are gods. Witness the pagan ritual of the Academy Awards, Abortion, a polluted entertainment media and we find Idolatry alive and well.

Idolatry cannot survive the challenge of true believers, though the odds seem overwhelming, but God is not mocked and believers must rise to proclaim the Kingdom, Power and Glory of God before it is too late.

PHASE CHANGE

One of the early concepts taught in Chemistry is that of phases. That is, an element or compound can exist in a number of phases that exhibit different properties, yet maintain its original structure. We can illustrate this simply by comparing the phase changes of water, the most abundant compound on earth. Water can exist as a solid, liquid or a gas.

Water is an amazing compound and its three properties are stunning and it is a function of the absolute temperature. At temperatures below 0° Centigrade, water exists as a solid. Its density is below 1 grams/cc and therefore ice floats. Ice demonstrates all the properties of a solid material related to compression, crystal structure and other properties of solids. Water exists as a liquid above 0° Centigrade and behaves as liquids, i.e. compressibility, ability to conform to its container, viscosity and density. The density of water is different to that of ice. In the vapor or gas phase, water exists as a gas having the properties of gases and behavior consistent with the Kinetic Theory of Gases.

The unusual properties of water are due to its molecular structure. Unlike carbon dioxide, which is a linear molecule (O=C=O), water has a bent configuration:

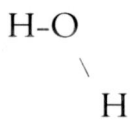

$$H-O$$
$$\backslash$$
$$H$$

This configuration is responsible for ice to float when it freezes. Had God not designed it this way, the oceans would freeze from the bottom up. The bent configuration also causes distortion of the electron cloud so water that has a molecular weight of 18 a.m.u boils at 100° C, while methane 16 a.m.u. boils at

-161° C. The difference is due to hydrogen bonding that does not exist in methane which is a symmetric molecule.

How can a single molecule behave in such independent ways yet still be a water molecule?

Christians can ask the same question. How can we have a Holy Trinity where we have three separate and individual entities, yet they belong to ONE? Well, consider the phases we just discussed and see that in the ice case, we can consider the Father, all powerful, solid and unmovable. With Jesus we have an all encompassing water, the Water of Life that covers every phase of life on earth and elsewhere. The Holy Spirit, invisible, just as water vapor is invisible, yet all powerful who controls our spiritual well being and thought processes.

What an amazing God we have who towers above all the Universe, yet is still concerned for our well being and Spiritual Salvation.

TALL TALE

The Bible continues to be the all time best seller in the world. It is not surprising that this is so, considering that the Creator is the author of its fundamentals, even though He used ghost writers like Moses, David, Luke, Paul and others. In spite of its constant popularity the Bible still has its share of detractors. These include those who deny the whole creation story, the divinity of Christ and the promises made to Abraham and his descendants. In addition, the miracles cited in the Old and New Testaments tend to confound the skeptics.

I am impressed by the many miracles in that some are based on simple chemistry while others require a faith to believe in the power of God. A good example of the former is the miracle that occurred at Lake Marah (Ex 15:25) where God commanded Moses to cast a tree into the waters to make the waters sweet. What really happened is that the log had lain in the sun and the cellulose was oxidized to form an ion exchange resin that sequestered the magnesium and calcium ions making the bitter water sweet. (Moses was the first Culligan man!).

While this has a logical explanation, it was God who set Moses up to carry out this miracle. Other miracles are more difficult to explain; raising Lazarus, the widow's son and feeding the 5,000 must be taken on faith. Other troubles for Bible detractors are the numerous prophecies that defy reason, yet in due time become reality. A number of examples will suffice. Isaiah predicted that a virgin would conceive and bear a child (Isa 7:14). This is an obvious contradiction to human nature, but nevertheless did occur as predicted. Micah (5:2) predicted that Jesus would be born in Bethlehem and though Mary and Joseph were from Nazareth, He was indeed born in Bethlehem. So, regardless how impossible a prophecy may appear, it does surely come to pass as written.

An interesting and somewhat troublesome prophecy is that due to Zecharias (Zech 14: 4) in which the prophet writes that His feet will stand on the Mount of Olives and the mountains will be divided from the East to the West. Such an image would require that Jesus would be a few thousand feet tall! Surely, the prophet is mistaken. However, considering all the other impossibilities in the Bible perhaps the prophet is correct. Our view of God and Christ are limited by our own narrow dimensions, yet God can hold the universe in His hand. In a recently published book "A Book of Angels" by Sophey Burnham, she describes an event that might make the above more plausible. Three Soviet astronauts had been in their space station for a long time, when they suddenly saw a bright orange light outside their spacecraft. On looking, they saw seven giant figures, with wings and halos. They appeared to be several hundred feet tall and their wings were as large as those on a jetliner. The band of angels followed the spacecraft for about ten minutes then vanished.

Twelve days later the seven angels reappeared and were seen by three more scientists who reported that they were "smiling as though they shared a glorious secret". The Soviets quashed the report, but word leaked out about this encounter in 1985. This could well explain the feasibility of Zechariah's prophecy. Considering the prophecies of Zechariah and the current turmoil in the Middle East and the world situation, we must soon realize that no man can put the world back in order but Christ Himself. Surely, in the Lord's Prayer, we say "Thy Kingdom Come" and we certainly must pray that it is soon and that we may see this prophecy fulfilled in our time.

WHO'S YOUR FRIEND?

I couldn't help but notice you recently. I don't know you personally, but for some reason, you have caught my eye and piqued my interest in you.

I have always been interested in the tableau of people and made a hobby of watching people and their behavior. Many people telegraph their inner feelings in their demeanor. In some cases I can detect the anger in their eyes or the anxiety in their expression. Many people project their mission; going from one place to another or coming from one place, then off to another. It seems that we are all preoccupied with our missions; many of which are of little value in themdelves, but which control our goings to and fro.

But, what interests me about you is that you seem to be at peace with yourself and your surroundings. When you enter a room, you seem to project, that is, radiate something, maybe an aura, which sets people at ease. You remind me of a priest I once knew, Father O'Brien, an author and professor at Notre Dame. One day I was returning from a trip and our plane to South Bend had been delayed. When we finally boarded the flight, you could cut the tension with a knife. People were fumbling with their overcoats, hats and luggage, impatient and actually hostile. Yet, after everyone was seated something strange happened. The last passenger to board was Father O'Brien. As he came down the aisle, he had a pleasant smile. He radiated an aura that spread calm all through that airplane's cabin. I felt that someone special had come aboard who brought and gave freely; tranquility and calm.

But, back to you!

In watching you I notice that you see a lot. I've observed you watching a flock of geese flying overhead with a real appreciation for their presence in your life. The way you look at plants, flowers, the clouds, the sunsets and even the rain, with a sincere appreciation for the Author of these great gifts. I always feel that you seem to be traveling with someone at your side. You don't act like you are alone and that someone has a very special place in your heart.

Does that someone speak to you?

Is He real? What is He like?

I wish I knew, because your whole life seems to be wrapped up with that silent, invisible companion, who makes you something so special.

Do I know your Friend? Would He talk to me too?

I wonder?

SECOND CHANCE

A few years ago, I read a most interesting book by Dr. Raymond A. Moody, Jr. entitled **"Life After Life"**. This book describes in graphic detail, numerous **Near Death Experiences (NDE)** of many of his patients. He became so intrigued by this that he began a deliberate study of this phenomenon. He later wrote another book in which he coined the term NDE to describe what happens to people who become clinically dead, then are revived.

The basic tale told by most NDE people is quite similar in its basics with a few variations. In sum, it involves leaving the body, seeing the surroundings where the death occurs, then going into a dark tunnel, then finding a source of light to which they migrate. As they reach the light some are accompanied by a **'Being of Light'** who radiates love and knowledge, there is a review of one's life in great detail, then the person is told that they must return, since their time is not yet. People who experience NDE are generally changed spiritually and have no fear of death and in many cases regret having come back to life.

A very good friend of mine died on the operating table during surgery and experienced a NDE. She later wrote me to describe the events which took place. Her parting comment was that we never need to fear death and how beautiful it is on the other side.

In looking over the literature of books published on this subject, I am amazed how much has been written. Many skeptics attribute this experience to nitrogen narcosis, carbon dioxide changes in the body and tricks which the brain plays to minimize the death process. Yet, there is so much to this that it is interesting that the scientific community has not given this more attention.

The other day as I was thinking about this, I began to wonder why people are given this glimpse of the other side and what it could possibly mean. In some writings, it is shown that there is an abundance of love and knowledge, peace and beauty there. There are also indications that humans experience life on earth as really death compared to that on the other side.

Euripides, an ancient sage, sums it up very well:

> **"Who knoweth, if to die**
> **Be but to live;**
> **And that called life by**
> **Mortals, be but death"**

It seems that a soul is required to go through life on earth to appreciate what is available in the after life.

This is not too far fetched. Consider Adam and Eve who had a paradise on earth, but had no knowledge of sin. Had they not fallen to the wiles of Satan, they might still be in the Garden of Eden. But, after the fall, they had to experience death, sin, illness, inhumanity and a host of plagues which are visited to life on earth.

Perhaps by making souls serve a life sentence on earth, the Creator has provided us a meaningful and unforgettable experience of what disobedience to God can mean for eternity. What better way to assure an eternity of peace and love when a soul is now experienced in the alternative choice. And, what a marvelous solution that God set it up this way, so that by following His way, we may enjoy an eternal Kingdom free of pain, hate and sin and live forever in an overwhelming state of peace, knowledge and above all - **LOVE**.

PART 3

ANIMAL STORIES

DOG STORY

The Bible is an all time Best Seller, a treasure of information and actually the Owner's Manual for Mankind. If all of the teachings of Jesus were included, there could not be enough books to contain it all (Jn 21:25). As a result, only key information is included and other information of importance must be added by concerned writers to expand on the wonders of God's Kingdom. Such a tale would include God's first creation that is not recorded in the Bible, but is clearly understandable from this essay.

When God pondered His first creation, He realized that such a creature must possess Love, Loyalty, Caring, Understanding and Devotion; a creature that would respect all the beautiful creatures, trees and plants in His Kingdom. After several design sketches He came up with a creature that had these properties. His first creation walked on four legs, was black and white and followed Him everywhere. God was so impressed with this creature He decided to give it a name. After pondering on this, God came up with a brilliant idea.

"I'll give Him my name spelled backwards," He said.

So this is how the Dog got its name.

Now Dog loved God very much. Dog looked like a Greyhound and went everywhere God went. When God left for work, Dog would follow Him to the gate and watch Him until he disappeared in the distance. Poor Dog was very lonely until the end of the day when He would see God coming up the path. God would be tired after a busy day creating the stars, galaxies and everything we now have. What pleased Him so much was to see Dog waiting eagerly for Him at the gate. Dog would wag his tail, bark and jump for joy. He would follow God into the house and stay with Him until bedtime. At night Dog would sleep at God's feet and also keep a careful ear for any strange sounds.

Everything was so good with God and Dog until one day God let Dog follow Him to work. Dog sniffed everything he could and ran circles around

God till He got to His office. One day, Dog was lying on the front step of God's office when an Archangel went by. Dog had not seen an Archangel before so he thought it would be fun to chase him. The Archangel ran for his life then finally took flight to escape Dog. Although Dog thought this was fun, he soon found out that this was not the proper thing to do. Several other angels also complained to God about Dog. God did not want to hurt Dog, so He decided to create a companion for Dog; especially since God was getting busier with all the creation work.

So God made man in His image and likeness as a companion for Dog. Dog and man got along well, even though Dog never forgot the wonderful times he had being so near his God. We say that "Dog is man's best friend" yet we should remember that the Dog is also God's best friend.

And so, this is how and why the dog was created. Though man has lost sight of the Creators' need for us to care for His Kingdom, the dog still has all the wonderful traits that God had required in His final design.

So the next time you see a beautiful dog remember that the dog was the first creature created and that the wonderful traits which God planned, Love, Loyalty, Dependability and Caring are all wrapped up in that creature with the wagging tail.

THE DOG KNEW

After I retired from Whirlpool Corporation in September 1991, Carol enrolled at Indiana University South Bend to pursue a degree in Piano Performance. Since I taught there it was convenient to taxi her to college and to help her in her in her new role as a college student.

Unfortunately, the faculty did not welcome her as a student and criticized her for pursuing a degree at her age and taking a place of other music students. One faculty member tried to convince her to quit. At any rate that was not a great start for her.

As time went on she excelled in Music History and Theory and began teaching piano at IUSB while attending college. In May 1998 she received her degree, with High Distinction, and also won the Prize for Music History and Theory.

The next year she was struck down by follicular thyroid cancer and told that she would never walk again. She had major surgery in South Bend and was confined there for some time.

A few years earlier Carol convinced me that we should get a dog…a greyhound. So we got WAKE, whose racing name was Horton's Wake. Wake was a very shy dog and we worked with her for some time to overcome her fear. Eventually, Wake was part of the household.

One day I was driving by the hospital on my way to purchase an air filter at the Toyota dealer. As we came down Notre Dame Avenue, Wake began to act up howling and barking until we were past the hospital. Wake knew that she was there.

The next week I obtained permission to bring Wake into the hospital. I put her in the car and drove down South Bend Avenue. As I turned onto Notre Dame Avenue, she went ballistic; howling, barking and whimpering. As I took her from the car she literally dragged me to the front door of the hospital. We got into the elevator to the fifth floor and she dragged me to Carol's room and jumped up on the bed.

The Dog Knew!

This is one of the most amazing stories associated with Carol's battle against cancer and one that proves that the Dog is one of God's most important creations and a creature that carries Love and Devotion with them everywhere they go.

BENNE

A prized guest in our home is Benne. Benne is a ten year old, black and white greyhound whose racing name was Benefit. Carol had originally brought three greys home, Benne, Miki and Sweetie. A week after Carol died Sweetie died and joined Carol in Paradise. Then in November Miki was stricken with kidney failure and could not walk. Dr. Wendell Garcia helped me carry her to the car and to see Dr. Anderson who euthanized Miki. This has been a sad year for losing our Miki and now I cling to Benne for companionship.

Last Sunday night I was preparing for bed and went through our usual procedure that includes cutting up some treats for Benne and getting into bed, which is a mattress on the floor that my good friend Donna gave me. After I get into bed, Benne will come over for her treats and sleeps next to me for the night. On this night Benne did not join me and I thought nothing about it assuming that she would join me during the night.

At 4 a.m. I noticed that Benne was not with me and I found her next to the TV set and hardly breathing. She was lifeless and very difficult to rouse. So, I slept next to her until morning and took her to the Mishawaka Animal Clinic. Dr. Anderson examined her and concluded that she had bone marrow cancer and should be euthanized. He took some blood samples and sent them off and kept Benne.

Later in the afternoon I decided to visit Benne so I drove to the clinic. They let me into the cage with Benne (they did not put a muzzle on me) and I spent some time with her. One of the ladies there suggested to Dr. Anderson that I take Benne home and spend the night with me. We could then euthanize her on Tuesday morning.

On Monday night before going to bed I took Benne into my arms and prayed that Jesus would help her. In the morning I took a number of pictures of Benne and then took her in.

When I reached the clinic, Dr. Anderson took over. About five minutes later, he returned shaking his head. All the tests came back negative and he could not believe it. He sent the samples to Purdue for further diagnosis and sent me home with Benne.

While Benne and I were praying, I had the feeling that Jesus had stopped what He was doing, listened and took action. (Jn. 14:13,14).

The folks at Mishawaka Animal Clinic project the love of God in dealing with their clients and share God's Love with us.

I am so grateful that I can still say, "Come on Benne, it's time for Bed. Thank you, Lord and Dr. Anderson.

BENNE
HOW LONG?

$\mathcal{J}$immy lived in the country away from the city. Near his home, there was a beautiful lake surrounded by a meadow, some woods and fields. Jimmy and his friend Willie loved to go down to the lake to watch all the animals, birds and fish. There were cardinals, crows, finches, robins and many other beautiful birds. Other creatures included butterflies; chipmunks, squirrels, rabbits and now and then he would see a fox.

One day as Jimmy and Willie were sitting by the lake watching all the action around them, they began to wonder how long it would take to create these creatures. For example, the butterflies are very delicate, but have beautiful colors. Wouldn't you think that it would take a long time to paint the beautiful colors on such an insect? What about a caterpillar? With all the legs on a caterpillar, it would surely take a long time to make one of these crawly creatures.

Willie did not know the answer, but his uncle Fred always came down to the lake to fish. "Why don't we ask him", Willie said. So the two boys got on their bikes and rode down to the edge of the lake where Uncle Fred was fishing.

"Do you know how long it takes to make some of these creatures" they asked Uncle Fred.

Uncle Fred was quiet for a few minutes, and then told them that these creatures are made by God in the time it takes for one of you to blink your eye. That is not much time is it? The boys were impressed!!

"But", Uncle Fred said, "There is one creature that takes a long time for God to make". "Do you know what animal that is?" asked Uncle Fred.

The boys thought about it for awhile and suggested a bird, a whale, a horse, but they were all wrong. Finally Uncle Fred told them that it was the Dog!!! It takes God eight hours to make a dog. The reason it takes so long is that God spends 7 hours and 59 minutes just to make the nose. After that God can quickly finish the job in less than a minute.

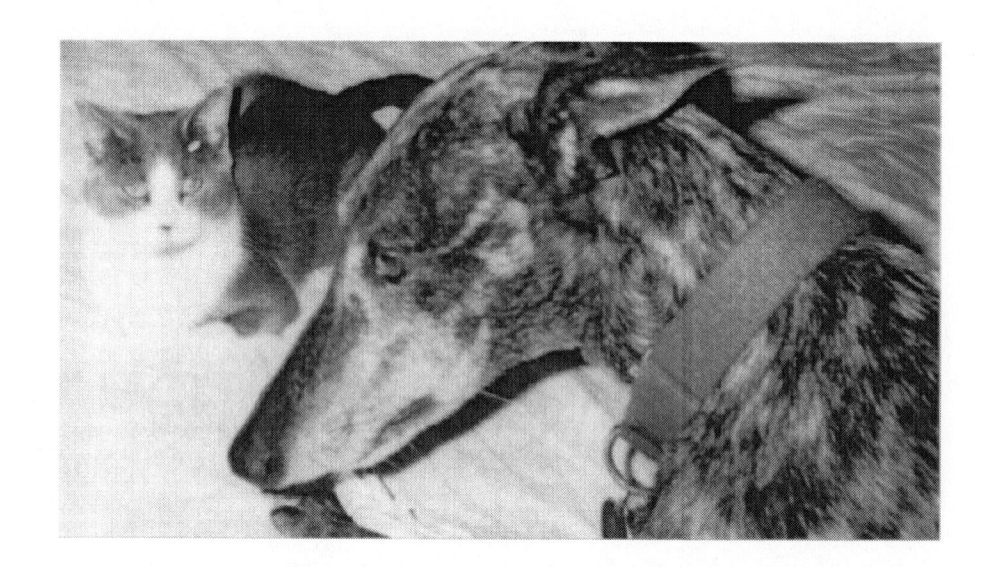

LOST SHEEP

This is a story of a young shepherd boy who lived many years ago. His name was Joel. Although he was only ten years old, he would go out with his father and older brother to tend their sheep. Joel loved to tend the sheep and to be out with them in the fields. During springtime he was especially fond of the wild flowers that grew. The sheep also liked spring because of the greener grass and the cool water that flowed from the mountain streams.

One day Joel's father called him to his side and told him that he had a surprise for him. Eagerly, he searched his father's eyes to see what the surprise would be. His father led him over behind a large rock. To Joel's surprise, he saw a tiny lamb with its mother. His father said to him, "Joel, since you love our sheep so much, I am going to give him to you". Joel was excited! He ran to the little lamb and took it into his arms. He cuddled the little wooly lamb in his arms and hugged it. His father warned him that he must take good care of the lamb and watch it at all times.

The little lamb had so much fur that Joel named him Wooly. Little Joel spent a lot of time playing with Wooly. He would run through the grass and hide, but the little lamb would always find him. Another time, he would hide behind a large rock and little Wooly would sneak up behind him and chew on his coat, much to Joel's surprise.

In the evening, Joel would tell his mother about all the things he and Wooly would do. Sometimes, his stories would sound as if he made them up, but his mother would laugh anyway and pretend they were real.

Everything seemed to be going so well for Joel and Wooly. But, Wooly was growing so fast that little Joel could hardly pick him up anymore. Wooly also would wander away from the flock looking for grass. Several times now Joel found him wandering up a high mountain. Joel would follow him and gently lead him back to the camp. But one day while Joel was helping his father,

He forgot about Wooly and the way he would go up the mountain. After working with the sheep all morning, they sat down to lunch. But, while Joel was eating and telling his father and brothers about what he and his lamb did, he suddenly noticed that Wooly was gone! Joel's little heart began to pound as he ran about looking for his beloved lamb. Finally, he decided that he must have gone up the mountain.

Joel took his little walking stick and some water in a goatskin bag and began the long climb up the mountain. Poor little Joel fell a number of times. It seemed that he would never find his good friend. After a long time, he reached the top of the mountain. He was now sobbing because he could not find his beloved lamb. Poor Joel finally threw himself on the ground and began to cry. Just then, he felt something pulling on his coat. He lifted up his head and through his tear filled eyes, he saw Wooly!

"Wooly", he cried, "where have you been?" He threw his arms around the lamb and hugged him for a long time. The little lamb was so happy he licked Joel's face.

"We must start for home now Wooly", Joel said, as he gave the lamb some water from his goat skin bag. But, just as he turned to start down the mountain, he saw four men climbing the mountain toward them. Joel was frightened. He had heard of robbers who lived in the mountains and now he was really scared.

"Why, oh why did Wooly have to run away and cause this trouble?" He said aloud.

Joel looked around and found two large rocks. He quickly led his lamb behind the rocks and told him to be quiet. The lamb sensed the danger and did as his little master ordered. Joel thought to himself that if he could hide until these robbers left, then he and Wooly could sneak back down the mountain to safety.

Joel put his arms around Wooly and held him very tightly. There was a tiny crack between the rocks which gave Joel a good view of the mountaintop and of the robbers coming up the trail. Joel's little heart pounded as the four men came closer. He wondered why they had climbed the mountain.

Finally, Joel held his breath. He whispered to be quiet just as the four men passed in front of the rock where they were hiding. Instead of going on, the men stopped there. Joel was frightened!

Would they find him and Wooly?

What did they want here?

Three of the men sat down and began talking to each other, while the other man stood looking up to the sky. Just then, something strange happened! The man who was looking up to heaven began to grow brighter. His light gray robe became as white as snow. His face became so bright, that Joel could not stand to look at his face. His three companions hid their faces under their cloaks. Joel too, pulled away from the crack in the rock and held his lamb more tightly.

Suddenly, he heard voices and he gathered up his courage to take another peek at what was going on. To his surprise, he now saw two very old men with long beards talking to the man whose clothes were as white as snow.

Joel thought about all the wild stories he told his family about his adventures with Wooly, but this was beyond his wildest dreams. He couldn't believe his eyes. Just then he saw a cloud coming and it covered the mountaintop. He heard a sound like thunder in the cloud. Joel hid his face. His little lamb was so still that Joel thought he was dead.

After a while, Joel looked again and saw that the two old men were gone and the other men were lying on the ground. The man who was standing appeared as he did before. Surely, he is no robber. Joel looked at his face and saw that he was a very kind, pleasant man. A sudden peace came over Joel; his little heart stopped pounding. Even little Wooly seemed to relax.

Joel watched as the man called to his companions to get up. As they came past the rock where Joel and Wooly were hiding, he heard the man say, "tell the vision to no one, until......".

Joel watched for a long time as they disappeared down the mountain. He then began to descend the mountain with his little friend. Joel wondered what that was. Surely, he could never tell anyone what he saw, for no one would believe him. But, he would never forget the gentle man who brought peace to him.
I wonder who He was?

THE LITTLE BUNNY

Once upon a time, long, long ago, there lived a little brown bunny. He had long ears and a big bushy tail. His mother called him Fluffy. He lived in a hole on the side of a hill with his brothers and sisters. When he was little, he spent a lot of time in the nest that his mother had made from soft grass and fur. Now and then he would wander out of the nest to a bright light at one end of his little home, but his mother would urge him back to the nest.

As he grew older, his mother warned him not to go out of the nest without her or his father.

"You must be careful of wolves and eagles" his mother warned.

She told him how some careless bunnies had been carried off by wolves and eagles. So, during the day, she told him to stay in the nest until the light went away. Then, under cover of darkness, his mother would lead the little bunnies out to eat the cool, sweet grasses that grew on the hillside. At any sign of danger, he and his brothers and sisters would scurry back to the safety of their little home.

As little Fluffy grew older, his mother would let he and his little brothers and sisters go out to the light at the end of their home. As he stepped out, he was surprised to see how bright and beautiful it was. He looked at the olive trees, tall cedars, and little cactus flowers. He saw many beautiful flowers and berries. As he looked around, he saw a funny animal looking at him. He had a long, curved tail and grey fur. Fluffy had never seen such an animal.

"What kind of an animal are you?" he asked. "Oh" said the little ball of fur, "I am a squirrel and my name is Henry".

Fluffy and Henry became good friends. Henry would climb trees and tell Fluffy of all he could see from on high. Fluffy and Henry also became friendly with the birds. There were gold finches, red cardinals, sparrows, hummingbirds, woodpeckers and robins. The birds liked Fluffy and would sing songs for him and also sound an alarm if a wolf or eagle were about.

Fluffy's mother would not let him wander far from the nest, even though there seemed to be better grass further from home. Toward evening, he would sit by the entrance to his home and watch the sunset. The birds would say goodnight and fly into the trees. Henry would climb a tree to his little house. As it grew darker, the stillness of the evening air would be broken with the sound of a cricket, followed by a tree toad until the whole night stillness would be drowned out by a symphony of sounds.

One evening as Fluffy was sitting outside his house, something unusual happened. He noticed the birds and all the animals hurrying over to a distant hill. They came from all directions; foxes, squirrels, deer, rabbits, field mice, chipmunks, donkeys and all you could name. They seemed to be in a hurry! Fluffy tried to find out where they were going, but they were all too busy to stop and chat with him. Finally, he asked his mother if he could go, but she refused. He did not want to disobey his mother. How he wanted to know what that was all about. Finally, he became tired and went to bed.

Several nights later, the same thing happened again. This time, even Henry went along, but again his mother would not let him go, even though he begged her. The next day Henry came by and Fluffy asked him what he saw; was there any danger?

"We went to see the King" Henry replied as he scurried up a tree. Fluffy also wanted to see the King so he told his mother about what Henry said. There was now a lot of talk in the animal community about this. Fluffy's mother went to visit Henry's mother, who had also gone to see the King.

So the next evening, Fluffy and his whole family decided to go to see the King over beyond the distant hill. Fluffy spent the afternoon cleaning his fur and washing his face. Fluffy was so excited as he hopped over the grass to the hill for he had never seen a King. As he approached the hill, he saw that it was a garden surrounded by olive trees. He stopped suddenly. Just before him stood a large rock and all the animals were gathered around the rock in a big semi-circle. The birds sat in the branches that hung low over the rock. Some of them had brought flowers for the King. But, there was no King. Fluffy sat down and looked around; the other animals were very quiet.

Fluffy was disappointed. He came so far just to see a rock - where was the King? He noticed a tired man in a grey robe walking up the hillside, obviously a gardener, but no King. After a while, the gardener came to and sat upon the rock.

The animals were delighted!

"Who's that?" he asked Henry.

"Why, it's the King!" Henry replied.

Just then, the birds started singing. Those who had brought flowers flew down from the olive branches and placed them at his feet. The King smiled and appeared to understand the animals. They watched him for a long time and the garden grew so peaceful. Fluffy then understood why all the animals came to see the King. He was overjoyed! Finally, a large deer turned away and as if it were a signal, the animals bid farewell and left for their homes.

After this, Fluffy would go to see the King whenever the animals came by. But, one day, he noticed that the animals were going to see the King but were very sad. Fluffy joined them, but as he reached the garden, he noticed that the King was not sitting on the rock, but was kneeling beside it. He was in agony; His face dripped with sweat and blood and He was very sad.

The animals were also crying! The big deer had tears running down his face and the birds did not sing. Fluffy was also sad. After a while, the animals were startled to see an angel standing by the King. They did not know what to make of this.

Suddenly, they heard noises as a large group of men bearing torches and carrying spears came toward the garden. The animals fled in fright.

This was indeed a sad day!

After that day, the animals never went to see the King again.

WHERE ARE THE DUCKS??

When I graduated from Notre Dame in 1959, we moved to our present home on Brick Road where we purchased a small home on two acres of woods. We soon began to clear some of the area and Carol planned her garden and flower beds.

One of our weekly rituals was to go to the Farmer's Market in South Bend on Saturday mornings to shop. The children enjoyed this event. One day we were walking through the market and a vendor spilled some strawberries from her display and we helped her retrieve the berries. This was our introduction to Arlene and Bill Stark and their children Beverly and Jerry. Arlene was grateful for our assistance and we soon became friends.

Arlene and Bill had a farm in Berrien Springs, Michigan and over time, they would invite us to visit and dinner. Their farm was on Lauer Road and consisted of peaches, raspberries, blueberries and during early spring pussy willows that they cut and sold as home decorations.

Jerry Stark also raised quail and ducks. He had a number of mallard ducks and they roamed the farm as if they owned it. Well, Carol thought that the ducks were so cute. Every time we visited she would admire the ducks and talk a lot about them. So on one occasion while visiting, Arlene suggested that she could give Carol some ducks for pets. Carol was elated and when we left that Sunday evening we took two pair of mallard ducks home.

Carol was excited!

So on Monday I was off to work and Carol let her ducks roam the back yard...she had her pet ducks and that made her happy...until things began to fall apart. When I came home from work she was teaching piano and told me that she was fed up with the ducks and I had to do something about them. You see she spent her afternoon trying to corral the poor ducks with little success.

Finally I asked, "Where are the ducks?

"In the garbage can", was her reply.

"Did you kill them?" "No".

So went out by the garage and there were these poor ducks sitting in the bottom of the garbage cans and very bewildered. So I built a pen in the back yard and placed the ducks in their pen where she could enjoy them. With time Carol's interest in ducks waned and chasing ducks lost its verve.

So one day we packed up the ducks and returned them to Arlene.

All was well now on Brick Road, but soon she began to tell me how much she loved donkeys. She pointed out that a true donkey has a cross on its back and legend tells us that is because the donkey carried Mary to Bethlehem.

Let's hope she doesn't want to get a donkey!

QUO VADIS?

In one of the legends about the early Christian Church we are told of the persecution that early Christians faced from the Romans and from the Orthodox Jews who were determined to crush this sect. As the persecution increased, the apostle Peter decided that it was time to get out of town ten minutes ahead of the posse`.

As Peter travelled out of Rome, he encountered Jesus Christ carrying a cross and Peter asked, "Quo Vadis?" Jesus responds that He is going back to be crucified again. It was at this point that Peter relented and returned to Rome to his eventual demise by being hanged upside down on a cross.

We in turn could ask the same question today as we witness cowardly leaders who don't lead; corrupt politicians accepting millions of dollars to keep them in office while failing to do their elected job. Our moral fiber is unraveling by the day as we now allow profanity in our daily discourse, on public TV and in talk shows. An egregious example is a TV video, sponsored by a radical group favoring immigration where they coached children to shout profanities and obscene gestures to illustrate their point. Our descent into the graveyard of failed nations is increasing exponentially!

MR. MOTT..NEVER MIND

When I started teaching at San Jose State College, I had made up my mind to remain a bachelor. This soon changed when one of my students, Carol Mott showed up in my Chemistry class. She was a bright student and one who made plans and carried them out. I soon learned that she had targeted me as 'the one' without my knowledge of the plot.

Soon she would show up at my office to go over problems. This was transparent since she was one of the top students in the class. In addition, Faculty rules prohibited dating students so that narrowed the choices. Carol was insistent and spent as much time with me as possible. To make matters worse, when she told her mother about me, her mother went ballistic and told her not to mess around with somebody with a name like mine.

Well, there are ways to get around the rules, so I used to make arrangements for my friend Glenn Baum to pick Carol up and transfer her to me. Her mother thought Glenn was a nice man and thought that he would be a better choice than that 'garlic eating Mexican' Tom who would never amount to anything.

After some time dating, things began to get serious. Carol wanted out of her home and used to stop by the St. Joseph Church every day and pray, "*Dear St. Joe, send me a beau; and never let him go*". So Carol and I decided that we would get married and she invited me to her home one Saturday to break the good news to her parents.

When I arrived at her home in Atherton, Carol was trimming some boxwood plants along the driveway and she started to pump me up to have courage to make the big announcement. So we walked to the back yard where her mother, her brother Irving and Mr. Mott were building a redwood fence.

Carol was behind me pushing a reluctant coward into action. Finally I said, "Mr. Mott! And without missing a stroke he shouted, "Irving, hand me that axe!" Mr. Mott then asked me what I wanted and I said, "Nothing", much to the dismay of Carol.

I received the Coward of the Year award for my bravery.

Sometime later, I did make the announcement and you should have heard Mrs. Mott who responded with a big, "WHAAAT?" that you could hear all the way to San Francisco.

At any rate, the business of love is a very dangerous one and people who practice it never know what to expect. I my case I had never ever thought that an axe would sabotage the best laid plans of a young lady in love.

God was certainly good to us.

UP THE STAIRS

During the early part of 2011, Carol began to lose the mobility in her right leg. After many tests we learned that she had a tumor pressing against the nerve that controlled that function. Doctors in South Bend declared that the tumor was inoperable. We then went to see Dr. Sasso at the Spine Center in Indianapolis who figured out a way to remove the tumor and straighten out her spine. The operation was a success and she slowly began to walk with a walker and a cane.

Because of her condition, we moved her to a bedroom on the first floor and she was bound and determined to walk again and wanted to return to our bedroom up stairs…an impossible task considering her condition.

One afternoon I came into the entry hall and found to my shock that she was standing at the top of the stairs holding onto the railing. She had done this all by herself and I asked her how she was able to accomplish the task.

As usual she had a simple solution to a complex problem. She told me that she would climb up three stairs, pause and say a Hail Mary then proceed to the next three stairs. So we adopted this procedure and it was my job to say the Hail Mary's each evening when we moved up to our bedroom. Her determination and Faith in God allowed her to cross many barriers that would prevent most people from even trying.

In our own climb up the stairs of life we encounter many obstacles that can be defeating, challenging or even impossible. Here is where we must first turn to God for our strength. We are reminded that *"The Lord is my strength and my Salvation"* and act on that belief no matter what.

Speaking of stair climbing, we had an Uncle Joe who was a dairyman and a real tough guy. People knew him by his name Joe or Double Rope because he always carried a rope with him so he could milk cows that might kick.

My brother Wally once had a dream that Double Rope had died and gone to heaven. St. Peter handed him a piece of chalk and told him to go back and write each of his sins on each step. Sometime later, Double Rope rang the bell and asked St. Peter for more chalk.

Let's hope we don't need more chalk.

TUESDAYS WITH MRS. MIRANDA

[This essay was written by Sarah Carleton, a student of Carol for Sarah's English class]

For eight years every Tuesday I have been taking piano lessons from Carol Miranda. She only stands four feet eleven inches, but from her small frame, life and energy pours out from her. Her seventy years of life have taught her many lessons which she has chosen to pass on to her students. Mrs. Miranda will share her wisdom with anyone who will listen and over the years I've learned through her stories and books and music history there are lessons to be learned.

Her piano studio is filled with books ranging from music theory to Jane Austin to one of her favorites <u>The Chronicles of Narnia.</u> Mrs. Miranda fondly refers to my weekly lesson as our book club. She has realized over the years that I am not going to be the next Mozart or Beethoven. Gradually our weekly meetings have turned into a time to talk about books and politics and life and less about chords and scales and quarter notes. We almost spent more time talking than playing. The lesson always starts with a story about her life lately. Recently Mrs. Miranda has been telling me of her latest read. Mrs. Miranda has decided to read through <u>The Book of Knowledge.</u> Each week she shares with me a new and interesting fact that she has learned from <u>The Book of Knowledge.</u>

When the lesson finally does begins Mrs. Miranda is never quick to criticize and is quite patient with me. As I fumble through the scales or try to find the right key or chord, Mrs. Miranda is there with words of encouragement and read to help me correct my mistakes. Mrs. Miranda realizes that each student is different and must treat them that way. While some students will move on to greatness, others like me are there to simply be able to enjoy the music we are able to play.

As the lesson draws to an end, Mrs. Miranda teaches me a lesson in generosity. She always has a gift to give me on the way out the door. Its cookies during the holiday season, a book she thinks I'll enjoy, some tomatoes from her garden or a final story for the way home. One of my favorite gifts she often shares with me is a trip through her extensive garden. Mrs. Miranda gives me a lesson in botany as she tells me the name of each lily we come across or a lesson in art when she shows me the newest statue her husband bought for her birthday. The garden tells me most about how much she cares for her students. She tends her students like she tends her garden. In each she plants a seed of knowledge and helps it grow so they can become better people.

Mrs. Miranda is a teacher that has been able to nurture her students to help them to grow into adults. As I take the next step in my life, I feel thankful that I have been able to have such a wonderful teacher. Mrs. Miranda has formed me into a better person and I'm glad to have listened to the wisdom she is able to provide me. My piano lessons aren't just piano lessons but have become life lessons.

THE VIOLIN LESSON

My wife of fifty eight years began teaching music when she was fourteen years old. She would offer piano lessons to the neighborhood children in Atherton, California for 25 cents a lesson. After I finished graduate school and moved into a home in Granger, Indiana, Carol began teaching again in our neighborhood. Her first student was Raymond Bennett, a boy who lived up the street from us. Eventually the word spread and she taught from 1955 until her death in 2011. Her last student was Dr. Wendell Garcia, a physician who studied violin with Carol.

Carol's students ranged in age from 6 years to 77 years old! She was able to diagnose the level of talent of her student and offer them music fit for their talent and maturity. Many of her students received first prizes in music competitions locally and at the State Competition. She also taught our children both violin and piano. Two of our children play in symphony orchestras today.

Carol also enjoyed great support from the Oriental Community and her fame among those was well known. When new members of the Oriental Community first arrive in the South Bend Area, they inquire of their friends about various services that they would need. A conversation would go like this:

New Arrival: Where do you bank?
Friend: First Bank.
New Arrival: Where do you shop?
Friend: Martin's or Meijers
New Arrival: Where do you find a music teacher?
Friend: Missy Melinda

So Carol and I enjoyed the fellowship of many friends.
Enter Dr. Garcia!

After arriving in the South Bend Area, Dr. Garcia decided to take up his violin lessons again and received a recommendation from a music store to ask

Carol. After interviewing him, Carol agreed to accept him in her studio. He would take a 45 minute lesson on Tuesdays, but many times his professional work would interfere with his lesson so Carol would schedule him for a Saturday make up lesson. Dr. Garcia, like Carol is a perfectionist and they both worked to make sure that his playing was up to her standards.

On a typical Saturday morning, I would go to the Farmer's Market, then to other shopping chores. As I left, Dr. Garcia would come in at 10:30 for his make-up lesson. When I returned about 12:15 I would still hear Paganini, i.e. Dr. Garcia, playing the violin. He was so determined to succeed he forgot that a 45 minute lesson did not last for two hours.

Carol's adult students have been a treasure to us and Dr. Garcia a valued treasure.

I can still hear Dr. Garcia, "Now let's go over this piece one more time!

FIRST AND LAST

In the gospel of Matthew, the apostle records an encounter with a rich man who is seeking Eternal Salvation and is told to sell all his wealth, give it to the poor and follow Jesus. The rich man refused and went away. At the conclusion of the discourse Jesus points out that the last will be first and the first last.

After Carol and I were married, we placed her Knabe Parlor Grand piano in storage. After I finished my army tour and graduate school, we were able to retrieve the piano and Carol decided to teach piano in the neighborhood.

He first student was Raymond Bennett, a neighbor. He studied with her for several years and in the ensuing years would stop by to visit. Meanwhile, Carol took on more students and taught piano, organ, violin and viola to students ranging from 5 to 75 years old.

Carol attended one year of college and dropped out when we married. When I retired, she enrolled at Indiana University South Bend majoring in piano performance. During her college experience she began to teach at IUSB and graduated with high distinction. Shortly after graduation, she was struck down by follicular thyroid cancer that had migrated to her spine so that she could not walk. After some surgeries and orthopedic procedures and the excellent care from Mary Pat Russ and the Grace of God, she was able to walk again.

In her later teaching years Carol acquired a number of adult students. One of her adult students was Dr. Wendell Garcia, a violin student. After interviewing him, she accepted him in her studio.

Because of his professional schedule, Dr. Garcia would miss a scheduled lesson and would require a makeup lesson usually on a Saturday or Sunday. This was the case on October 2, 2011 when he arrived at 4 p.m. for such a lesson. At the end of his lesson, he told Carol that he was going home to retrieve his stethoscope. When he returned and examined her, he told me to take her to the

Emergency Hospital; since he felt it was better to go then instead of tomorrow morning at 5 a.m. Carol died three days later.

Dr. Garcia was her last student!

Last Spring I was having lunch with Dr. Garcia at a local restaurant when Ray Bennett came in with a friend. I introduced him to Dr. Garcia and pointed out the coincidence of meeting Carol's first and last student.

LAST CHANCE

The Presidential election of 2016 is to be the most important election in the history of this once great nation and could be our last election!

Ever since the Insiders plotted to take over this country in 1910 at Jekyll Island, we have been on a downward spiral to leading this nation to the trash heap of history. Shortly after Jekyll Island we began to receive the benefits of the One Worlders who gave us the Income Tax, perpetual war, entitlements, reckless spending and racial strife. Attempts to reign in this disastrous course have been unsuccessful as we slowly began to dumb down education, lower morality, spend recklessly and appoint a congress who became subservient to the lobbyists.

As we descended lower we were given leaders like Jimmy Carter whose administration gave us the Iranian Hostage Crisis, unusually high interest rates and high taxes. The national attitude was that of malaise as citizens were blamed by Carter, for the sad national demise. There was despair throughout the nation.

Then there was Ronald Reagan! His election ended the Iranian Crisis, turned the economy around, lowered taxes and gave Americans a reason to be proud of our great country. His impact lasted for some time, he gave us leadership again. Then we went back to electing weak candidates and the congress was stacked with people beholden to lobbyists and self interests. The final nail in our national coffin was the election of Barack Hussein Obama, a leaderless president who proceeded to complete the task started on Jekyll Island over a hundred years ago.

Today we are faced with a dangerous situation. The Democrats have anointed Hillary Clinton to be our next president. She represents all that is wrong with a presidential candidate; an ordained liar and a very questionable leader. Meanwhile, the Republicans, the more conservative wing of the Democratic Party and leaderless, have fielded a number of candidates who are falling over each other to see who can be assured to continue the downfall of America.

EXCEPT ONE!!

In Donald Trump we have a leader in the mold of Ronald Reagan, but with the most impressive trail of undeniable success in Business, a God fearing family man, a man who loves his country and a leader with a vision. He has trampled over the candidates who dance around the issues and has laid out a clear plan to make America right again. He is such a contrast to the candidates who make a statement, are challenged, and quickly rush to apologize. Have you heard Donald Trump back up over his statements in the face of criticism?

Mr. Trump's approach to solving the many problems in our country is the only hope we have left to save this great nation.

Should the establishment vigilantes derail his train, and they are working on that, America is finished!

This is your last chance America! Take it!

SUMMARY

This book contains a number of short essays that express concern for the demise of this great nation as we rush to the Graveyard of Nations. The thought of running through a graveyard at night is terrifying for any young child and more importantly for this once great nation that has succumbed to the siren call of those who would seek our destruction. Our Constitution, founded upon Christian Principles by wise men, that recognized that power comes from Above and that the gifts of God must be cherished and defended if we are to succeed in enjoying the benefits of a good life provided by the Grace of our Creator. Evil men have been jealous of the gifts we have received and have plotted our demise since the creation of America. The essays address moral decline, the failure of churches to do their jobs, the abortion disgrace, state of government failures and reflections of good friends who make up the treasures of life. Personal tales of the author's trip through life are presented. It is the authors desire that some of the suggestions presented make sense and be worthy of responding in a positive way to save this great country.

ACKNOWLEDGEMENT

The author is especially grateful for the support and love of our dear friends who have stood by Carol and me during our journey through life. Special thanks to Irene and George Pospolita, Donna Kash, Joyce Anne Kidd, Christine Forry, Dr. Wendell Garcia, Mary Pat Russ and Thomas K. Weinberg. I am especially grateful to Alice Hoover for spiritual support and for her guidance on Scriptural topics. Sincere appreciation for Carol's many students and their families, ALL OF HER TREASURES.

ABOUT THE AUTHOR

Thomas J. Miranda is a native of Hawaii and has been active in the field of Polymer Chemistry and Coatings Technology for over forty years. His achievements as scientist, inventor, author and lecturer are well documented in polymer synthesis, heterogeneous catalysis, polymer stabilization, water soluble polymers, emulsion technology and radiation chemistry.

The author was born on a sugar plantation, Ewa Mill, Oahu and grew up in Honolulu and lived there until almost a year after the Pearl Harbor bombing that he witnessed. He moved to California, graduated from San Jose State College with an AB and MA in Physical Sciences, taught there for one year, then served in the Army Chemical Corps. He received a PhD in Organic Chemistry from the University of Notre Dame in Polymer Chemistry where he was the W.R. Grace Research Fellow and an MSBA from Indiana University where he taught as an Adjunct Assistant Professor of Chemistry over a twenty three year period.

His business experiences include Director of Research for the O'Brien Corporation and Staff Scientist at the Whirlpool Corporation. He served as President of the Paint Research Institute, Technical Editor for the Federation of Societies for Coatings Technology's *Journal of Coatings Technology* for twenty years and Editor of the Monograph Series on Coatings Technology. He served as an Industrial Consultant in the Materials Science area.

He received a number of local and National Awards for Outstanding Scientific Accomplishment and the Outstanding Business Alumnus Award from the Business School of Indiana University South Bend.

He has published over 50 papers, book chapters and is the author of 13 United States Patents, and two books, *Growing up in Hawaii, and A Bedside Reader.*